PRAISE FOR **TRUST**

"Dig into the pages of this book with confidence. *Trust God's Promises* walks through the Scripture to identify ten magnificent promises that are more certain than the ground upon which we stand. Dr. Wayne Dickard has walked through these promises with integrity in his own life, and his voice is that of a powerful preacher whose insight helps us find rich application and abundant hope!"

Joe Hopkins, President
Campbellsville University, Kentucky

"Dr. Wayne Dickard is an incredible man of integrity. His latest book is full of practical truths to sustain, strengthen and encourage his readers. This book is inspiriting and much needed for today's culture. It is written with passion and wisdom to inspire readers to seek after the many promises of God. It is delivered in such a way to propel one's own walk forward with the Lord. There is not another author whom I had rather read who expounds upon the promises of God like author and pastor Wayne Dickard. It is a must-read about God's faithfulness and how you can apply these nuggets of truth to your life."

Julie Hammett Cannon
Author, wife, mother of three, public school counselor

"*Trust God's Promises* is filled with powerful and touching real-life stories from Wayne Dickard's years of ministry, but it is not about its author — it is about his Savior Jesus. Every chapter is based on the Word of God, which contains His 'great and precious promises,' and our God has not, cannot and will not lie. You will be encouraged and challenged by this book. It will take you back to some better and happier times in life and ministry, but it is as relevant as today's newscast. While our world is changing every day, our God is the same yesterday, today and forever. This book is a timely reminder that all the promises of God are YES and AMEN in Jesus!"

Gary Hollingsworth
Executive Director-Treasurer
South Carolina Baptist Convention

TRUST
GOD'S
PROMISES

TRUST GOD'S PROMISES

WAYNE DICKARD

 COURIER PUBLISHING

Trust God's Promises

Courier Publishing
100 Manly Street
Greenville, S.C. 29601
864-232-8736
www.courierpublishing.com

Printed in the United States of America.

DEDICATION

It gives me great pleasure to dedicate this book to the Judson C. Dickard family. I am grateful to God for His goodness upon the Dickard ancestry.

There is a long spiritual heritage dating back several centuries upon this lineage. The Dickard family immigrated to the United States from Germany more than a century ago. One of our ancestors, Peter Dickard, was instrumental in planting a church in Newberry, South Carolina, in the nineteenth century, and there is a historical land marker there commemorating that special place. Since those early years, the Dickard family has been known for actively supporting local churches.

My mother's ancestors immigrated to the United States from Northern France. She was from the Leroy lineage. The Leroy family was also comprised of active church people.

Since 1860, at least one of my mother's or father's ancestors in each generation became a preacher of the gospel. Currently, my brother Robert preaches and serves as a director of missions. My brother Randall is an active Baptist layman in Anderson. Two sisters, Louise and Inez, are active in Easley churches. Daniel, our son, pastors the Friendly Avenue Baptist Church in Greensboro, North Carolina. My wife, Anita, is a retired public school teacher and is my rock and help in the ministry. She constantly serves at my side and has worked wherever she was needed in the churches I have served. Our son Stephen is a member of a Baptist church. Christ and His church have been a big part of the Dickard heritage, and it makes me happy to dedicate this book to them.

I am thrilled over God's calling for salvation and service to the Dickard family. May this bloodline always appreciate the spiritual legacy God has given and may they stand strong in His Church.

Anita and I have six grandchildren: Kylie, Kenna, Conrad, Kesyd, Bradley and Carolina. Three of them have been saved and baptized into Baptist churches. We are praying for the other three to be saved as they reach the age of accountability. Our family has benefited from so many of the great promises of God.

Because of God's goodness and grace, I dedicate this book to the Dickard family in hopes that it will bless them and others.

FOREWORD

In this book, Anderson University alumnus Dr. Wayne Dickard shares rich insight into ten promises God has made to His people. More than words in an ancient text, the promises of God are active, real, and reliable. Unlike fallible men and women, God is truthful and unchanging, therefore He can be trusted to fulfill His promises in His timing and perfect way. The author reminds us that God always follows through on His Word — His holy bond. God fulfills His promises sometimes in ways that are beyond our understanding, but fulfill them He does!

Dr. Wayne D. Dickard, and his wife Anita, a retired public school educator, have led lives of humility and authentic servanthood. For more than thirty years, Wayne has lovingly shepherded congregations in churches with Anita's unfailing support and shared labor. In addition to his pastoral responsibilities, Wayne has served in various Southern Baptist leadership roles, including as president of the South Carolina

Baptist Convention and as a trustee of Anderson University. Throughout this book, anecdotes and examples from Wayne's life, including his ministry, family and marriage, serve to illustrate the certainty and permanency of God's promises.

This exceedingly readable and enjoyable book will be a blessing to all Christians. Have you felt crushed under the weight of trials in your life? This book is for you. Has your heart been overwhelmed with grief or pain? This book is for you. Do you ever wonder how you can face tomorrow because you feel so alone today? This book is for you. Have you faced a difficult decision, unsure of the wisest way forward? This book is for you. Wayne details how each of the Lord's promises are available, abundant, and enduring.

Apologist C.S. Lewis said, "God can't give us peace and happiness apart from Himself because there is no such thing. If we find ourselves with a desire that nothing in this world can satisfy, the most probable explanation is that we were made for another world."

The living Creator-God cares so much for us

that He not only gave us the incomparable gift of salvation through faith in his son, Jesus Christ, He gave us these wonderful promises that give us confidence to not only confront the challenges of this life, but overcome them for time and eternity.

As president of Anderson University, a Christian university in Anderson, South Carolina, we equip students with knowledge, skills, and values for a lifetime of service to God and humanity. While teaching and learning are our main activities, the most important thing we do is to bear witness to Jesus Christ and help our students understand His purpose for their lives. I continuously encourage our students to consider two central questions as they prepare for life ahead. What am I animated and gifted to do, and what kind of person do I want to be?

We can boldly seek after God's will for our lives because, upon our beckoning, God's promises open in His timing like gifts before our eyes, giving us purpose, revelation, and joy. Yes, God has a purpose for you and me. He walks alongside us as we faithfully pursue His will and the delight of His heart. I trust you will find the words and truths in this book to be a source of matchless satisfaction and hope.

Evans P. Whitaker, Ph.D.

Anderson, South Carolina

PREFACE

God is rich in honor and keeps His promises to all generations. His eternal words will never fail. Like the pledge from the rainbow in the sky, His promises are always reliable and lasting for every age of life. They are valuable in times of peace and times of trouble. The prophet Nahum stated, "God is good, a stronghold in a day of trouble and He knows those who trust in him" (Nahum 1:7). God makes promises throughout Scripture to demonstrate His love and compassion for those who trust in Him. He is the sovereign God who is plush in mercies and slow to anger. The Apostle Paul declared, "All the promises of God are yes in Christ Jesus" (2 Corinthians 1:20).

The psalmist proclaimed, "Trust the Lord" (Psalm 4:5), and the Apostle Paul said, "Trust in the living God" (1 Timothy 4:10). That indicates we should believe and then expect all the promises made by Him to come through. At age fourteen I knelt on my knees and asked Jesus to be my Savior and Lord. A few days later, on May 5th, 1967, I walked down the aisle at Corinth Baptist Church in Easley, South Carolina, and told the preacher about my decision to follow Jesus. I professed then and still believe today that Jesus is the Son of God who came to save sinners from their sins. By faith I received Jesus as the master of my life. While I have failed Him many times, I can confess that He has never failed me. He promised to save me if I would call upon His name. I did just that, and it was a life-changing moment in this sinner's life. That day, He fulfilled His promise to save (Romans 10:13). Since that encounter, I have come to believe that every promise made in God's Word is true. If a single promise from God were false, then none could be trusted. However, God speaks truth, and His promises are reliable. We can expect Him to fulfill everything He has pledged to us.

This book was written to remind its reader about the many wonderful assurances God has given to us. I will elaborate on ten promises found in God's inerrant Word that express the trustworthiness of those promises. This project begins with the messianic promise revealed with the birth of Jesus and concludes with the eschatological promise that Jesus will come again. We will review the bond of His Love and probe His offer of help to every Christian along life's journey. We will talk about His willingness to save the lost and His promise never to leave us alone. We will advocate that His promises are abundant, His truths are eternal and each one will be kept.

Martin M. Hyzer shared a story about Abraham Lincoln, the sixteenth president of the United States. Lincoln was riding in a coach with one of his military officers when that officer offered President Lincoln a drink of whiskey, which he declined. Later, the officer offered Lincoln a cigar, which he also declined. The president, sensing the curiosity of the officer, told him why he did not drink or smoke. Lincoln explained that when he was nine years old, his mother called him to her bedside and said, "Abe, the doctor tells me that I am not going to get well. I want you to be a good boy and promise me before I go that you will never use alcohol or tobacco." Lincoln said, "I promised my mom that I would honor her request, and up until this hour I have kept that promise! Would you advise me to break that promise?" The officer put his hand on the president's shoulder and said, "Mr. Lincoln, I would not have you break that promise for the world."[1] While Lincoln was faithful to the promise he made to his mother, there is one who is far greater and more reliable, honorable and trustworthy than the sixteenth president. Our God has kept, or will keep, every promise He has made. No one else can lay claim to that record. God has never, and will never, break His promises.

Wayne Dickard

February 2022

TABLE OF CONTENTS

TRUST
GOD'S
PROMISES

CHAPTER 1

GOD PROMISED A MESSIAH

But He was wounded for our transgressions, He was bruised for our iniquities: the chastisement of our peace was upon Him; and by His stripes we are healed. (Isaiah 53:5)

God is loving, compassionate, trustworthy and sure, which should cause all His creation to trust His promises. There are many wonderful guarantees recorded in Scripture that give optimism to every generation. A favorite promise of mine is found in Proverbs 3:5-6, which states, "Trust in the Lord with all your heart, and lean not unto your own understanding. In all your ways acknowledge Him, and He will direct your paths." Other examples of His promises can be found in multiple Bible texts. Hebrews 13:5 declares, "I will never leave you, nor forsake you." The Apostle Paul affirms in Romans 10:13, "Whosoever calls upon the name of the Lord shall be saved." In Psalm 23, the psalmist declares, "The Lord is my shepherd, I shall not want." On and on I could go recounting the great promises of the Bible, but perhaps one of the most cherished promises for believers was written by the prophet Isaiah: "For unto us a Child is born, Unto us a Son is given; And the government shall be upon His shoulder. And His name shall be called Wonderful, Counselor, Mighty God, Everlasting Father, the Prince of Peace." Isaiah later expanded on that promise when he wrote, "But He was wounded for our transgressions, He was bruised for our iniquities, the chastisement of our peace was upon Him, and by His stripes we are healed."

Isaiah's announcements were referring to God's Son, our Savior, Jesus Christ. Isaiah was boldly telling the world that God would send a messiah, or "deliverer." The psalmist expounded upon Isaiah's words when he wrote, "The Lord is my rock, my fortress and my deliverer" (Psalm 18:2). The term for "deliverer" is akin to the New Testament term "Christ," which comes from a Greek word meaning, "Anointed One." Isaiah's announcement of a future Savior gives the world a glimpse of God's Anointed Son who would one day save His people from their sins. The Anointed One, says Isaiah, was "wounded for our transgressions, He was bruised for our iniquities: the chastisement of our peace was upon Him and with His stripes are we healed." Certainly, Isaiah was writing about the Messiah Jesus Christ. Thus, the term messiah became a customary designation for the Son of David, which was fulfilled in Jesus of Nazareth.

God's covenant with the world included a propitiation with God. That big ole word, "propitiation," means God's act of appeasing for the sins of a sinner, and it is akin to the word "atonement," which was introduced into the English language in 1526 by William Tyndale in his translation and explanation of reconciliation. God desired to reconcile His people unto Himself, and that is why He sent His Son to be our deliverer and Messiah.

From 1984-1994, I was privileged to pastor the Homeland Park Baptist Church in Anderson, South Carolina. That was my first pastorate after seminary. I loved that church and the people of Homeland Park. The church grew, and I grew as a pastor. One Sunday afternoon, I was sitting in the office looking over my notes for the evening service while my wife led the children's choir practice. My phone rang, and someone on the other end said, "Preacher Wayne, there has been a terrible accident, and you need to come to the Anderson Memorial Hospital." I learned that a grandmother was bringing her grandchildren to choir practice and was involved in a fiery car wreck. I later learned that as this grandmother passed through an intersection on a country road, her car was hit, knocking it into an open field. A passerby reached the wreckage and began pulling victims from the burning automobile. First, he got the grandmother out. He then rescued a third-grader. Before he could get a sixth-grader out of the wreckage, the car exploded. That sixth-grade girl perished in the wreckage. The third-grader was airlifted to the Cincinnati, Ohio, burn center. The grandmother was airlifted to the Charleston, South Carolina, burn center. I flew to Cincinnati the next week to visit the third-grader and his family. I later drove to the Charleston burn center to visit the grandmother. I will never forget the words of that grandmother. Dressed in all the required protective clothing, I was allowed into the burn unit. While I looked into that grandmother's face, she said, "I am so glad that someone came by to deliver me." I reflected on that statement and wrote it down, because that similarly describes what God did for His people. He sent His Son to deliver us from sin, wreckage, and hell. Hallelujah, what a Savior!

That grandmother in that burn unit was genuinely expressing her gratitude over a stranger who delivered her from a fiery wreckage. Her gratitude reminds me that all men should show appreciation for God's "outstretched arms" of deliverance. He reached out through Jesus to offer help for the hurting and to deliver the wounded. God promised the world a messiah, and He delivered on that promise.

Remember, God keeps His promises. Daniel wrote about God's promised messiah in Daniel 9:25 when he declared that one day the world's messiah would come. The prophet Micah talked about God's promise in Micah 5:5 when he stated that the Deliverer would be born in Bethlehem. Jeremiah relayed God's promise in Jeremiah 23:5-6 when he explained that a king would come from the lineage of David and deliver His people. Jeremiah said, "Behold, the days are coming, says the Lord, that I will raise to David a branch of righteousness. A king shall reign, prosper, and execute judgment and righteousness in the earth. In His days, Judah will be saved, and Israel will dwell safely."

We know the promise for a messiah is as old as Moses, because Moses explained God's promise for a messiah by saying, "I will rescue you from your bondage and will redeem you with an outstretched arm" (Exodus 6:6). The "arm of the Lord" is an Old Testament expression that evokes a picture of God's caring hand being extended toward the earth. That phrase is used again in Exodus 15:16 when Israel sang a song claiming victory over the Philistines. The phrase "arm of the Lord" is once again used in Deuteronomy 15:5, when Moses told Israel to remember that they were slaves in Egypt and the Lord your God brought you out with a mighty hand and "outstretched arm." The terminology is used in both First and Second Kings. Solomon proclaimed in 1 Kings 8:42: "People will come from a far country, for they will hear about your great name, your strong hand and your outstretched arm."

Yes, God has always extended His hand and arm of help toward His people. The best demonstration of His "outstretched arm" toward us was seen when He sent His Son and our Savior as the world's Messiah. The Apostle John was referring to that event when he declared, "He was in the world, and the world was made by him, and the world knew him not. He came unto his own and his own received him not. But as many as received him, to them gave he power to become the sons of God, even to them that believe on his name" (John 1:10-12). Thus, God sent Jesus, as the fulfillment of His promise of an "outstretched arm."

The God who extended His arms to Moses, Jeremiah, Solomon, Daniel, John, and a host of others extends His arms to you and me. If that were not true, I would never have written this book. If that were not so, I never would have preached all those sermons about Jesus! If that were not true, then I would never have taught that truth to my family. But it is true! God extends His love and favor toward us. When the world is against you, God's arms are extended toward you. When your family is against you, God's hand is reaching toward you. When you struggle with addictions, God's arm is reaching out for you. When you go through the trials of life, God's arms are extended toward you. God is good, and He cares about the minute details of your life. He sees you when you are down, and He rejoices over you when you are up. Nothing can separate you from the love of God. When the struggles of life seem to overwhelm you, reach up to God, for He is reaching down to you. His steadfast arms are extended toward the earth.

So how do we recognize the messiah? What does He look like? Will He be a political leader? Which kingdom will He rule? These are but a few of the questions that people asked while pondering God's promise of a messiah. Isaiah was the prophet God chose to answer those questions about the Deliverer. Now remember, it was Isaiah who said, "Unto us a child is born, unto us a Son is given" (Isaiah 9:6). Later, he provided a much deeper and clearer understanding about the messiah's outward form. He connected the phrase "arm of the Lord" with the revealed Promised One and asked, "Who has believed our report and to whom has the arm of the Lord been revealed?" (Isaiah 53:1). While connecting these two thoughts, he explained that the messiah would grow up "as a tender plant," which means the plant will come out of the ground tender and fragile but will grow into a strong vine.

Let me illustrate with a personal story. My wife and I love okra. Last spring, we went to a local seed store and bought some okra seeds. We initially placed the seeds in small pods of soil. When we planted those slips, some looked very scrawny and frail. We actually thought some of them would die. But we watered and cared for the plants, and to our amazement they grew larger than the other plants we had seeded. By the end of the summer those scrawny plants were so tall we had to use a step ladder to cut the okra from the stalk. Never had we seen okra grow so high. That is but a feeble effort to describe what Isaiah was explaining to the world.

Jesus was born in a manger in Bethlehem. He looked like anything but a king. He was just a tender plant. He was a root out of the ground, but, oh, how He grew. His beginning did not resemble that of a king. Yet He was the King of kings and Ruler of all rulers. He was the Promised One and a reminder to us that God always keeps His promises.

Isaiah proceeded further with His description of the Promised One by saying, "He has no form of comeliness, and when we see Him there is no beauty that we should desire Him" (Isaiah 53:2). The word comeliness means splendor and beauty. It gives the idea of appearance. The term is likened to an ornament with no special beauty. This does not mean that Jesus was an unattractive person; it simply means that God was not sending a beauty contestant but rather a Savior, Ruler and King. When Jesus came as a fulfillment of Isaiah's prophecy, He was unique and well-reported in every way. He was the Messiah that was promised. He was the Anointed One and Savior, which was promised. The "arm of the Lord" was specifically and meticulously seen through the coming of the Lion from the tribe of Judah. His name was Jesus, the name above every name.

Isaiah furthered the world's understanding by stating, "He will be despised and rejected of men" (Isaiah 53:3). And, in the very first chapter of his Gospel, John expounded about Jesus: "He came unto his own, but his own received him not, but to as many as received him, to them He gave power to become the children of God" (John 1:12). Jesus was despised by the Pharisees, the Sadducees and even the Herodians. The government wanted to kill him, the religious leaders tried to entrap Him, and the Jewish people rejected Him. Jesus completely and perfectly resembled Isaiah's description of the messiah. From the cradle to the grave, He followed His Father's plan. He was on mission from heaven to bring salvation to the world. He was about His Father's business, fulfilling His Father's promise.

Isaiah finished his description of the Promised One by saying, "He was wounded for our transgressions." I do not have enough pages in this book to express the pain and grief the Son of God endured. However, Martin Luther expressed it well when he said "the punishment was laid on him so that we can have peace."[2] Jesus was beaten, cursed, rejected, spat upon, crucified, and buried. He received the stripes that belonged to sinners. He willingly gave Himself for the sins of the world. He sacrificed Himself to reconcile the world to His Father. He was the Promise that God made to a sinful world.

In 1903 the Wright Brothers, in Kitty Hawk, North Carolina, were able to fly an airplane for the first time. They were so excited about their accomplishment, and sent a telegram to their sister, which read, "Success four flights ... with engine power alone average speed through air 31 miles longest 57 seconds inform press home Christmas."[3] Katherine quickly took the telegram to the local newspaper and showed it to the editor. The editor read it and said, "Nice, the boys will be home for Christmas."[4] The editor missed the main message, which was, the Wright brothers actually flew in an airplane for the first time. Like the editor, we, too, often miss the main message about Jesus. He came as the Promised One! He came to save sinners from their sins. God sent His Son to be our Deliverer. He is the Messiah, the Christ, the Anointed One. He is the fulfillment of God's promise. So regardless of how many issues swirl around us, we must not let minor things crowd out the major thing. God sent a Savior, and Jesus is His name. Trust God's Promise. His arm is extended. His Son came, and His salvation is provided.

To conclude this chapter permit me to mention some applications one might learn from this promise:

• First, God is for us, and if God is for us, then who can be against us? His hand of favor is extended toward His people, and He offers help to anyone who reaches back toward Him.

• Second, there are many wonderful proofs found in Scripture that reveal Jesus as the promised Messiah. He was the child that was born and the Son that was given. Jesus is the Wonderful Counselor and Mighty God.

• Finally, the promised Messiah was revealed in Jesus, and if one wants to fellowship with God, they must go to Him through the Promised One.

CHAPTER 2

FOR GOD SO LOVED THE WORLD

For God so loved the world that He gave His only begotten Son, that whoever believes in Him should not perish but have everlasting life. (John 3:16)

The most popular promise in the Bible is found in the most popular verse in the Bible, which declares, "For God so loved the world that He gave His only begotten Son, that whoever believes in Him should not perish, but have everlasting life" (John 3:16). That verse has been called the gospel in a verse, and the gospel in a nutshell. It reveals God's promise of love to the whole world. It further promised that anyone and everyone who will trust in God's Son, Jesus, will not perish in hell but instead live with God forever in heaven.

An article was published in Ron Beckham's Friday Study Ministries in which he related a story about a young boy in Chicago:

> In the city of Chicago, one cold, dark night, a blizzard was setting in. A little boy was selling newspapers on the corner. The little boy was so cold that he was not trying to sell many newspapers. He walked up to a police officer and said, "Mister, you wouldn't happen to know where a cold boy could find a warm place to sleep tonight would you? You see, I sleep in a box up around the corner and down the alley and it's awful cold in there for tonight. Sure, would be nice to have a warm place to stay."
>
> The policeman looked down at the little boy and said, "You go down the street to that big white house and knock on the door. When they come to the door you must say 'John 3:16' and they will let you

in." So, he did as he was instructed.

He walked up the steps and knocked on the door, A lady answered. He looked up and said, "John 3:16." The lady said, "Come on in, son." She took him in, and she sat him down in a split-bottom rocker in front of a great big old fireplace, and she went off. The boy sat there for a while and thought to himself, "John 3:16 … I don't understand it, but it makes a cold boy warm."

Later she came back and asked him, "Are you hungry?" He said, "Well just a little. I haven't eaten in a couple of days, and I guess I could use a little bit of food." The lady took him in the kitchen and sat him down to a table full of wonderful food. He ate and ate until he couldn't eat any more. Then he thought to himself, "John 3:16 … boy, I sure don't understand it, but it sure does make a hungry boy full."

She took him upstairs to a bathroom and to a huge bathtub filled with warm water. He sat in their tub and soaked. He thought to himself, "John 3:16 … I sure don't understand it but it sure does makes a dirty boy clean."

"You know, I've not had a real bath in my whole life. The only bath I have had was in front of that big old fire hydrant as they flushed it out."

The lady came back in and got him. She took him to a room and tucked him into a big old feather bed, pulled the covers up around his neck and kissed him goodnight. As he lay there in the darkness and looked out the window at the snow coming down on the cold night, he thought to himself, "John 3:16 … I don't understand it, but it sure makes a tired boy rested."

The next morning, the lady came back up and took him back down to the same table full of food. After he ate, she asked him, "Do you understand John 3:16?" He said, "No, ma'am." She then took her Bible and explained John 3:16. Right there in front of that fire, he gave his life to Jesus. He sat there and thought to himself,

"I don't understand John 3:16, but it sure makes a lost boy feel safe."[5]

There are several truths that I would like to mention regarding the promises made to us in John 3:16. First, God loves us unconditionally. Love is the strongest emotion known to man and is defined as "feeling deep affection or emotions for a person."[6] There is nothing anyone can do to make God love them more, and there is nothing one can do to make God love them less. God is love, and He showers His creation with His unique, immense and never-ending affection.

The love of God is limitless. The word "so" speaks to the size of God's love. His love is so deep and wide, so high and strong, that it caused Him to give His Son to reconcile this lost, dark and sinful world to Himself. His love is so rich that the brightest of the bright cannot totally comprehend or understand it. It cannot be duplicated, because it is a one-of-a-kind love. Thus, no one can ever love like Jesus loves.

God made and rules His world. He has such a deep affection for it that He gave His Son to be the sacrifice in order to save it. His care for the world should make us both humble and grateful. However, God's one-of-a-kind love was not limited to one person or one group; it was given to, and included, all people. The scope of God's love is seen in the word "world" because it is translated from the word "cosmos" and refers to the whole universe. It gives the idea that God did not limit or exclude His love from any part, or anyone.

When I was in preschool, our Sunday school teachers would lead our class in singing a song with lyrics: "Red and yellow, black and white, they are precious in His sight, Jesus loves the little children of the world."[7] Both young and old should know that the love of Jesus covers the whole world, and not just some parts.

It is not God's will for anyone to perish. He wants all people and people groups to know Jesus through repentance and faith. Jesus died for the sins of the whole world and the whole world can be saved.

God's promise also speaks to the sway of His love which is seen in the term "that." The word indicates the size and scope of God's love. It is so enormous that it brought about an action by God. He saw the world separated from Him by its sinful actions and it moved His compassionate heart to do something about it. He was moved to end the world's state of separation. God's action was painful and expensive. It required Him to do something that brought grief to His heart. It required His only Son Jesus to be sacrificed. No one can know just how it hurt the heart of God to do what He did, but He was swayed to act out of a heart of love for mankind. Only His son could pay the world's sin-debt. The Apostle Paul explained it well when he said that Jesus was the propitiation for our sins. That word means that Jesus came to appease God for a debt that was owed.

The love of God never grows old! His love will never be revoked and will never lose its power. Jesus simply loves every person. God's love is as certain as the sun that shines down on us. You can trust His claim regarding His affection because He proved His endearment by giving His only Son.

There are many names in the Bible that reveal the greatness of God. The second aspect of this promise is its gift, and that gift has a name. The name is Jesus. Names are important. In the Old Testament, the name Jehovah is used 6,800 times and means "The Ever-Living One." The name Elohim is used over 2,400 times and means "God is mighty to declare." The term El Shaddai is used over 300 times and means "God rules over everything." The name Jehovah Jireh is used only one time (Genesis 22:14) and means "God provides." But there is one name that excels them all, and that name is Jesus. Paul said, "There is no other name under heaven given among men whereby we must be saved" (Acts 4:12). He also said, "At the name of Jesus every knee shall bow, and every tongue confess that Jesus is Lord" (Philippians 2:10). Names are important, and God chose the name Jesus to give to His Son. The name Jesus means "God is salvation," and salvation is exactly what God sent His Son to give.

Song writers compose lyrics about the name of Jesus, preachers preach about Jesus, and people around the world pray in the name of Jesus. His name is an exalted name because Jesus is an exalted gift. His name is both an exalted gift and an eternal gift. So what does this promise mean to a lost sinner? The answer is that it brings both inward and outward change to a person's life. Paul declared, "If any man is in Christ, he is a new creature, old things are passed away and all things become new" (2 Corinthians 5:17). Hell is not an option for the child of God. When one comes to know Christ, heaven becomes their eternal destiny. The Scripture teaches that to be absent from the body is to be present with the Lord. That means when a Christian dies, he immediately goes into the presence of Jesus. Jesus said, "I am going to prepare a place for you, and if I go and prepare a place for you, I will come to receive you unto myself that where I am there you shall be also" (John 14:3). Paul tells us that our citizenship is in heaven and not in this world (Philippians 3:20). Therefore, heaven will be our eternal home and we will dwell in the house of the Lord forever. Thus, one of the wonderful changes that takes place in a believer's life is his destiny.

This promise also means that hell can never be experienced by a Christian. Hell is an awful place. The Bible speaks more about hell than it does about heaven. The phrase "will not perish" means that a saved person will never go to that dreadful place. So what makes it so dreadful? The space available in the pages of this book will not permit me to explain all its dread, but I will mention a few things about hell. First, it is described as a place of outer darkness. Darkness is the domain of the Devil, while Jesus is the light of the world. Can you imagine what an eternity in darkness would resemble? The darkness of hell is an impossibility for a Christian but a certainty for lost sinners. Hell is also referred to as a place of fire and pain. Perhaps no pain is greater than the pain that comes from a burn. Fire burns from the outside in, but Jesus changes from the inside out. The pain that is caused by the fire in hell is why the Scripture declares that there will be wailing and gnashing of teeth. The pains of hell are indescribable, and that truth alone should cause believers to rejoice over the impossibility of going to such an awful place. However, the greatest pain of hell will be separation from God. To be cut off from the One who loves us the most would be torment in itself.

Jesus is an exalted gift because He changes our destiny. He also changes one's behavior here on earth. Old things are passed away and all things become new. The things we loved before we believed in Jesus are the things we loathed after we believed. The places we went before we believed are the places we stay away from after we believed. The language we used before we believed is no longer a part of our vocabulary. A person's heart is changed when he is saved, and, as a result, his behavior is changed.

I was blessed to pastor the Northbrook Baptist Church in Boiling Springs, South Carolina, for almost ten years. The church experienced great growth, and I was able to lead that church to build a new sanctuary and educational building. After moving into the new building, church members worked for months in the evenings and on Saturdays to convert the old sanctuary into a very nice fellowship hall. One Saturday afternoon, after having worked all day on the construction project, I walked over to my study in the new building to look over my sermon notes for the next day. While sitting there in my study, the Spirit of God, in a quiet, still, small voice, nudged me to go visit Chuck Johnson. Chuck had attended services the previous Sunday. I argued with God about making that visit. I was dirty and tired, with paint all over my clothes, but I could not get away from the persuasion of God to go visit Chuck Johnson. I knew that Chuck was not a fan of preachers or churches. He had attended his first worship service the previous Sunday. Christ and His church had never been a part of Chuck's life.

I got into my car and made my way across town to Chuck's house. I rang the doorbell and Chuck opened the door. He and his family had just returned from a Clemson football game. Chuck politely invited me into their living room, where he and I sat and talked about Jesus. Chuck was a volunteer worker on the Mike Duvall race team. Chuck said to me, "Mike told me last night that one day a preacher is going to knock on my door and talk to me about Jesus, but I did not think it would be so soon." I knew God was at work. I told Chuck how he could repent and believe on the Lord and be saved. He said, "I want to be saved." That day, Chuck got on his knees and asked Jesus to come into his heart and save his soul. That was a life-changing moment for Chuck. I left and made my way back toward my office, rejoicing in the Lord.

A couple of weeks passed, and Chuck came to my office at church to ask if he could talk with me. He began to talk about how salvation had changed so many things in his life. One of the changes was his vocabulary. Chuck owned and ran his own business. They made various building products. He supervised strong-minded and sometimes foul-mouthed employees. Chuck told me he had lost half of his vocabulary because he did not want to cuss anymore. I smiled and told Chuck refraining from using foul language was a good sign that Jesus had in fact come into his heart. I was able to help him understand how God's Holy Spirit changes a believer's sinful behavior. Remember: Old things are passed away, and all things become new.

Not only does God's eternal gift change one's destiny and behavior, but it also changes one's countenance. God instills joy into a believer's heart, and it radiates to his outside countenance. That new outside countenance reflects the love of God to others. To illustrate this truth, let me tell you a story about some prospectors in the hills of California. They were panning for gold when one found an unusual stone. Upon breaking it open he saw that it contained gold. They then continued working eagerly until they had discovered an abundance of the precious metal. They shouted, "We found it! We are rich!" After running out of supplies, the three decided to go into town to restock. But before leaving camp, they covenanted together to not tell anyone about their find. After buying the needed goods, they all started back to camp and noticed a group of men following. One of the prospectors asked the men, "Where are y'all going?" To which the men said, "With you three, because y'all have found gold." "Why do you say that?" asked one of the prospectors. "Because it shows on your faces," replied one of the followers.[8] Likewise, Jesus shows on the face of the person who receives Him. Jesus changes a person's countenance!

The last thing I would like to mention regarding this promise is the part that uses the term "everlasting life." John 3:16 declares that a believer will not perish but have everlasting life. That means that there is no end to the life with Jesus. There is no end to forever. Our lifespan on earth is relatively short. Life is like a vapor, declared Solomon. It quickly vanishes away. It seems like only yesterday that I was playing ball with my two boys in the backyard, but they are both grown now. That reminds me just how short life is. However, it is long enough to meet Jesus and be saved. It doesn't take long to believe in God's promises, but the results and blessings are eternal. Fellowship with God is a blessing and a promise that everyone can trust.

There are several truths that I would like to mention regarding the promises made to us in John 3:16. First, God loves us unconditionally. Love is the strongest emotion known to man and is defined as "feeling deep affection or emotions for a person."[9] There is nothing anyone can do to make God love them more, and there is nothing one can do to make God love them less.

My wife often sings a song which is a modern rendering of the old hymn, "The Love of God." The lyrics are:

> The love of God is greater far than tongue or pen can ever tell. It goes beyond the highest star and reaches to the lowest hell. The guilty pair, bow down with care, God gave his Son to win. His erring child he reconciled and pardoned from his sin.[10]

Those song lyrics remind us of the love promise that God gave to the world He created.

"For God so loved the world that He gave His only begotten son, that whosoever, believes in Him, shall not perish but have everlasting life." Permit me to mention several applications one might draw from this promise:

• First, God loves us unconditionally. There is nothing one can do to earn or buy His love. Love is who He is.

• Second, the love of God is eternal. His love has always been and will always be. Nothing can separate us from the love of God. No wife nor husband, no son nor daughter, no sibling nor friend, can remove those who are in Christ Jesus from fellowship with God.

• Finally, the love of God offers a place in heaven for anyone who opens their heart's door to the Savior. He stands at the door and knocks, waiting and wanting the door to be opened to Him.

CHAPTER 3

SALVATION AND FAMILY

Believe on the Lord Jesus Christ, and you will be saved,
you and your household. (Acts 16:31)

Luke shares one of God's greatest promises while writing the Book of Acts. He declares, "Believe on the Lord Jesus, and Thou shall be saved and thy house." Since entering the ministry, I have used this verse on my personal business cards. Those cards containing that promise have been left at homes and businesses and with acquaintances for decades.

That promise provides hope for every family and reminds the reader about God and His salvation. Over the length of this chapter, I will attempt to establish the benefits that Acts 16:31 supplies to those who accept it by faith.

The apostle Paul was en route to Asia when he received his "Macedonian call." God's angel directed Paul to Macedonia, which is in Europe, rather than continuing his journey to Asia. He graciously obeyed God and changed directions. Servants through the ages have accepted such redirection in ministry and life. Paul believed that he should go to Asia, but God said no, go to Europe instead. Thus, obedience to God's "no" mandates are just as important as being obedient to God's "go" mandates. Paul changed course and made his way toward Europe. He arrived in Philippi, which is a part of the Macedonia province. When the Sabbath came, Paul and his team searched for a place to worship. Worship on the Lord's Day was important to Paul, and should be important to every saint of God. Faith that does not take you to church and worship may not take you to heaven. The Scripture teaches that believers should not forsake the assembling together with other believers. Since there was no temple in Philippi, this group went to the riverside to fulfill the ceremonial requirement of Judaism. At the river, they found a group of ladies and a few men worshipping. One of the ladies was Lydia, a businesswoman, who made her living selling dyes. The mission team shared the gospel with that group, and some were saved, including Lydia. After her conversion, Lydia invited Paul and his mission team to abide at her house while they did evangelistic work in Philippi. They accepted her invitation and were very happy to have a base from which to operate and share the gospel in that city. However, leaders of the city and those who peddled vice were frightened by the radical changes they saw taking place in their city. The turning of many from paganism to Christianity began to affect the income levels of those who sold pagan trinkets. The change in the new converts was easily noticed by those who had not become followers of Jesus. The spiritual movement in Philippi became so great that the city leaders threatened Paul and his missionary team. Ultimately, Paul and the team were arrested, beaten, and thrown into prison because city leaders deemed them a threat to their culture.

Shortly after Paul and his group were placed in prison, an earthquake shook the prison cells, and the jail doors swung open. The guard who had been given the responsibility of guarding Paul was about to commit suicide when Paul said to him, "Do yourself no harm" (Acts 16:28). He assured the guard that the whole mission team was present. The guard was so moved by their actions and their calm behavior that he washed and bandaged their wounds. It was during that life-changing moment that the jailor asked Paul, "What must I do to be saved?" (Acts 16:30). His question was answered by the preacher with these words: "Believe on the Lord Jesus, and thou shall be saved, and thy house" (Acts 16:31).

This jailer was a hardened sinner. His very job required him to work among some of the most wicked and sinful men in the province. Most of the men he guarded had done some bad deeds, which rightfully landed them in jail. However, the jailor's hard shell did not prevent him from hearing and believing the gospel. So, what was it that God used to penetrate such a hard-shelled sinner?

First, God used the testimony of those faithful Jesus-followers. Paul and Silas had been stripped, beaten and unjustly imprisoned. While in excruciating pain, they were chained in the inner part of the prison. That section of the jail was probably dark, damp and dangerous. The conditions around those Christian believers did not deprive them of having peace in their hearts. We know this because they sang and worshipped God at the midnight hour. Their singing could be heard throughout the prison and made an impression on the hardened jailer. While the prisoners were singing about Jesus, the prison building began to shake. God sent an earthquake to assist the mission team in their witnessing endeavor. Isn't that just like God, to show up when we need Him? These men could have escaped, but they chose to stay put. God was at work, and these men wanted to be where He was working.

Their actions caused the prison guard to realize

these preachers had something he was lacking and desperately needed. It caused him to yearn for the peace that he saw in his prisoners. His wonderment led him to ask, "What must I do to be saved?" God used personal testimonies of song and speech to bring this man under conviction. Never underestimate the power of a testimony. It sometimes reaches where sermons cannot.

The second thing God used to bring the jailer under conviction was an earthquake. This earthquake was so strong that it opened the doors but did not cause the building to fall on the inmates. Again, that is just like God: to give us just what we need, no more and no less. The jail, which was sturdily built and con-structed to last, suddenly began to shake. The doors violently flung open. The stocks that were built to hold even the strongest of men broke like match stems. Paul and Silas were free to flee but decided to stay. Why? They were already inwardly free, and the physical freedom on the outside would not match the inward freedom they already possessed; God set them free when He saved them. Something more powerful than an earthquake had broken Paul's bondage years earlier on a road called Damascus. It was on that road that Paul had his life-changing moment. On that road, he received Jesus as his Savior and Lord. It was because of that life-changing moment that Paul's countenance, conduct, conversation, and character all changed. From then on, he wanted to be like Jesus. It was his changed life that God used to cause the jailer to want inward freedom. The jailer knew something was different about these men. He came to realize it was no accident these men were put under his care and into his jail. It was no accident they were telling him about Jesus. God used these men's changed lives to bring the calloused jailer to his own life-changing moment. The jailer was quick to know that he wanted what Paul and the others had.

The greatest compliment that I have received came from a professing atheist. For months, this atheist visited our church services. He came because his wife and son had been saved and were attending. I visited him in hopes of leading him to Christ. He was a nuclear physicist who had just retired and moved to our city. His wife and son had become active followers of Christ. He told me that he did not believe what his son and wife had come to believe. However, he kept periodically coming to church on Sunday mornings. One day I made a return visit. I said to that professing atheist, "You tell me that you are an atheist, but you come to church, you occasionally sing, and you seem to enjoy the services. If you do not believe in God, why do you come?" He said to me, "Preacher, I do not believe what you believe or what you preach. But I believe that you believe it, and I like to hear you tell it." That atheist has yet to be saved. However, he is in no way beyond the reach of God's salvation. God used men like Paul and Silas to melt the heart of a Philippian jailer, and when His servants needed assistance, He sent an earthquake. Neither that jailer, nor that atheist, nor any other breathing soul is outside the reach of God's grace. May we be found faithful testifying and preaching about God's grace.

A third thing God used to reach the jailer was the threat by the magistrates. He was told that he must guard the prisoners, and if they escaped then he would pay for it with his own life. That was an understood rule for prison guards. When Paul and Silas chose not to escape and remained in their cell, their actions spared the jailer's life. He was astounded that these men who had endured unjust beatings and torturous stocks, when given the opportunity, would not leave. Their actions so touched the jailer that he was willing to listen to what they had to say. Our talk must match our walk in order for sinners to listen to what Christians have to say. Had Paul and his group left their post, as uncomfortable as it was, they would have forfeited their opportunity to tell the jailer how to be saved. God used their steadfastness to bring conviction to that jailer. May God never find us AWOL from our post of service. These men were right where they needed to be in order to be used by God.

God majors on putting His servants and tools where He needs them. Let me explain. Many years ago,

I was teaching history in the public school system while serving as a volunteer youth leader at the East Gaffney Baptist Church. Our pastor, Dr. George Lockaby, invited Dr. Carl Bates, pastor of First Baptist Church of Charlotte, North Carolina, to lead those revival services at East Gaffney. One night Dr. Bates shared about how he came to receive Jesus as his Savior. He was broken and empty, sitting in a hotel room in New Orleans with a loaded gun pointed at his head. He sat, contemplating whether to live or die. While holding that gun in his hand, wrestling through one of the most difficult struggles of his life, he opened a desk drawer and found a Gideons Bible. He took that Bible from that drawer and began to read about the love of God. Dr. Bates laid down the gun, bowed his head and asked Jesus to come into his heart and change his life. He chose life in Jesus, not death. He later chose to surrender his life to preaching the gospel. It was during that revival, led by Dr. Bates, that I walked the aisle and told my pastor that God had spoken to my heart about preaching the gospel. Not knowing where God might take me or how God might choose to use me, I knew I had to answer His call to service. While everyone does not endure the hardships that Paul and Silas endured, nor do they go through the struggles Dr. Bates endured, every saved sinner does experience a life-changing moment. That encounter leads them from death to life in Jesus. Every convert gains peace of heart that is beyond understanding. Serving Jesus may take you down a hard path, or it may take you up a pleasant trail, but it will always take you to the right path. The jailer was saved when he heard God's promise relayed to him through Paul. He said, "Believe on the Lord Jesus, and you shall be saved, and your house."

A final truth learned about this promise: Salvation ends not at the heart of the saved sinner, but it reaches others throughout one's whole house. That is a promise from God. So how does salvation affect one's family? Paul said to the jailer, "Believe on the Lord Jesus, and you will be saved, and your house." The term "and your house" does not mean that a child, wife, parent, or brother can go to heaven on the coattails of a relative. Salvation is never imparted by the actions of another, and no one can be saved in absentia. You may have the godliest mom or dad alive and still die as a lost sinner. Jesus said to Nicodemus, "You must be born again" (John 3:3). Salvation is uniquely personal. You must put your faith in Jesus to save you from your sins. When someone asks Jesus to save him, He will save him. The Scripture declares, "For whosoever calls upon the name of the Lord shall be saved" (Romans 10:13). Paul was telling the jailer that you and your whole family can place your faith in Jesus and be saved. Some take the position that Paul's statement meant that the jailer's influence would lead his family to Jesus. And while a man does exert great influence over his relatives, his relationship with Jesus does not automatically impart salvation to anyone. Salvation is a personal matter between a holy God and a sinful man. This statement matches the theology given to the Ephesian believers. Paul said, "By grace through faith are you saved, and that not of yourselves. It is a gift of

God, not of works lest anyone should boast" (Ephesians 2:8-9). Grace through faith is the venue though which everyone is saved.

I am a "whosoever will" preacher. I do not believe anyone is outside the scope of God's grace. Peter tells us that it is not God's will that anyone should perish, but that all come to repentance.

Scripture tells us that broad is the way that leads to destruction, and narrow is the way that leads to everlasting life (Matthew 7:13). I take that to mean more will be lost than will be saved. Yet God loves us and invites everyone to be saved. Paul was relaying to the jailer that his whole family could place their faith in Jesus, and He would save them from their sins.

During my first full-time pastorate, I shared the gospel with a young man in hopes of leading him to Christ. I asked, "If you were standing before God and He asked, 'Why should I let you into my heaven?' what would you say?" That young man said, "I know I am going to heaven because my momma was a Christian." Sadly, he was very sincere but very wrong. Too many believe that a place in heaven can be reserved through a relative's faith. Paul in no way was implying that to the jailer. He was conveying that his family could be saved.

Another time while witnessing I asked a man if he would like to ask Jesus into his heart (Ephesians 3:17) and he said, "I am going to heaven because I am a member of the lodge." Well, a lodge or any other organization can never provide you a ticket to heaven. You must confess Jesus with your mouth and believe in your heart that God raised Jesus from the dead, and you will be saved (Romans 10:8-10).

Again, salvation is uniquely personal. It is free to anyone who will come to Jesus by faith. That promise, made through the mouth of the Apostle Paul and recorded by the pen of Luke in Acts 16:31, should bring joy and gladness to the hearts of both the saved and the lost. You can trust the pledge of God when He said, "Believe in the Lord Jesus and you shall be saved, and your household." Hallelujah, what a promise!

To conclude this chapter permit me to offer

some applications that one might draw from this promise:

• First, anyone can be saved. Whether a cultured sinner like Lydia or a calloused sinner like the jailer, no one is beyond the grace of God.

• Second, there is great influence by a father which extends to his whole household. When dad gets saved, the chances are great that others in his house will follow Jesus, as well.

• Finally, do not underestimate the visible and invisible ways in which God can come beside His servants to offer help. It is not always in the form of an earthquake that God helps the efforts of His people. He more often uses subtle ways to assist their witnessing efforts.

CHAPTER 4

I AM WITH YOU

For I am with you, and no one will attack you to hurt you; for I have many people in this city. (Acts 18:10)

The promises found in Acts 18:10-11 revolve around the life and ministry of the Apostle Paul while serving in the city of Athens, Greece. God spoke to him in a night vision and said, "Do not be afraid, but speak and do not keep silent; for I am with you, and no one will attack you to hurt you; for I have many people in this city." God gave both instructions and assurances to Paul at a low point in his ministry.

It has been my experience that God gives His servants what they need when they need it to keep them on the firing line of ministry. This promise to

Paul has been claimed and used to comfort countless pastors and servants in every generation. It was during my first full-time pastorate that this verse became personal and valuable to me. I had to make some decisions that were not popular with some church members. Thirteen people left the church that Sunday out of a congregation of 140-150 average weekly worshippers. I believed then and now that the decision I made was for the betterment of the church ministry. Yet such decisions usually come at a cost to the pastor and rest on the pastor's desk. The pressures that follow unpopular decisions can become immense. I prayed and sought God's help and was reassured by God's Spirit that I had made the right decision.

On Friday of that week, a disgruntled staff member requested a meeting with the deacon chairman. The chairman agreed, and invited me to attend the meeting. The staff member laid out his case to the deacon chairman and me. I sat mostly silent, which is highly unusual for me. Near the end of the meeting the deacon chairman said to the disgruntled staff member, "It appears to me that you do not want to change and do what you are told." That ended the meeting!

While such experiences are unpleasant, God uses them to reaffirm His support for His servants. I knew God was at work in that matter. It helped me to see that He had not brought this young and inexperienced pastor to a new church in a new city only to be forsaken.

The events of the following Sunday further assured me of God's abiding help and presence. He confirmed to me that I was not alone. Having thirteen members leave the church at the start of my ministry was not what I had in mind. However, when I gave the invitation the very next Sunday, fourteen people joined the church.

Since that experience, the promise of God's presence has brought strength to my life. The Lord said to Paul, "You are not alone, and no one will attack you to hurt you." Many other servants through the ages have claimed that passage as a constant reminder of God's goodness and presence. In crisis moments, His promises become large and timely. They bring a calm confidence to moments of chaos. Trusting God's promises brings steps of growth to one's life!

The Apostle Paul was facing one of his crisis moments when he arrived in Corinth. The Spirit of the Lord had directed him to that city for the purpose of preaching the gospel. Corinth was one of the two most important cities in Greece at that time. It was about forty miles from Athens and possessed a population of approximately 700,000 people, more than half of whom were slaves, shoppers, seamen and merchants from other parts of the world. The presence of so many noncitizens was due to their skid system, which moved ships across land from one body of water to another. At Corinth, ships were transported approximately four miles via skids from the Adriatic Sea to the Aegean Sea. While a ship was being transferred over land, passengers would often disembark for a time of shopping and pleasure in the city. Thus, commerce flourished, drawing workers, merchants, seamen and foreigners to Corinth. It was to that multicultural city Paul was sent to serve. He was a gifted tentmaker and could make and sell his product, as needed, in places like Corinth.

When Paul arrived in Corinth, he was emotionally and physically drained. He felt like a failure because of the unfair and hostile treatment he had received in Mars Hill. People had laughed at his message and called him a babbler. That caused him to feel lowly and discouraged. Few words sting a preacher more than verbal rejection of his preaching. No doubt, the Mars Hill experience stung the pioneer preacher. Paul was a man who spoke several languages and had been educated by the best of the best. He had been trained at the feet of Gamaliel, the elder. He had sat on the Sanhedrin council, which was the highest council in Israel. He had preached to thousands of listeners before arriving at Mars Hill. However, his message and ministry were mocked by the elites in Athens. That treatment made him feel deserted and alone.

Paul preached and traveled throughout Europe,

which caused fatigue. Because of a lack of funds, his ministry often required him to be bi-vocational. When church support ran low, he preached and worked at tent-making in various locations. Both tent-making and evangelism were laborious tasks. Churches should have a healthy respect for bi-vocational preachers. Long and rigorous schedules had worn on the preacher and his ministry team. It seems the Devil works hardest when people are at their lowest moments. The Apostle Paul was fatigued and challenged in Corinth.

Paul was somewhat fearful. Convincing himself that he was alone in a megacity caused him to be frightful. Fear can be an ugly companion that destroys one's confidence. He was wondering how he and his few ministry helpers could make a difference in such a large city. Thinking God had only the preacher, alone, to get the gospel out to that great city was a wrong assumption. Paul was assuming a burden that was not his to own. Both his and our responsibility is to share the gospel, but depend on God for the increase. God does not call lone rangers to the ministry, but willing servants. Thinking you are the only tool God has is a ploy of the Devil. Don't entertain those types of thoughts, because they limit God's power to work in your life. He has servants that you and I don't see or know.

Paul was frustrated because of the size of the city and wondered if he could make a difference in such a large population. How could he find a platform on which to preach, and could he be safe given his most recent experience in Mars Hill? These and other feelings flooded his heart. The mocking elite were left behind in Athens and Mars Hill, but their behavior had made an impact on that servant's heart. Critical words and bad experiences are some of the hardest things to get past in ministry. He was having one of his lowest moments, but Jesus came to his rescue. By reassuring Paul he was not alone, Jesus gave him a promise that changed the direction of his ministry. Jesus said, "I am with you." What a promise! When you are fearful, Jesus is with you. When you feel deserted, He is there. When you feel frustrated and overwhelmed, Jesus comes to your aid. When you are frightened by what may happen, know this: Jesus is your protector. He sees around the bend of the road and knows all the dangers that might befall us!

Jesus gave four promises, all wrapped in one encounter. The phrase, "Jesus spoke," tells us that Jesus had some clear directives for His frightened preacher. When Paul needed a word, God gave him directions. It is exciting to hear from the Lord. Hearing from the Lord challenges the listener, and it does not have to be an audible voice that conveys the message. When Jesus speaks, our hearts are melted, our fears are erased, and our frustrations end. We then become happy and blissful because of the fellowship we find in Him. There is nothing more refreshing than getting a word from the Lord. That kind of divine encounter can alter the direction of one's life and ministry — and one's eternity. Oh, how we need to have regular fellowship with God, and that fellowship can be found through prayer and in the Holy Scripture.

Part one of Jesus' promise guaranteed His presence: "I am with you." This statement confirmed to Paul that, indeed, he was not alone in ministry, preaching and evangelism. If you have a lone ranger complex, get rid of it! That is a tool of the Devil because, if the Devil can convince you that you are alone, then he has convinced you that God has abandoned you — and God never abandons His children. Whether it is a mental, physical, or financial crisis you are facing, just know you are not alone. As the Lord was with Paul during his crisis moments, so will He be with you.

The second part of Jesus' promise centered around God's protective hand: "No man will attack you to hurt you." Jesus reassured the preacher that nothing would happen to bring personal harm to him. God would not allow it. Our battles are not our own; they belong to God. He will protect those who serve Him. He journeys with us through the low moments of life and brings us out safely on the other side. And on the other side of our loneliness and despair we will see the results of the protective hand of God. Peter,

Paul and John experienced times of hurt. They encountered feelings of despair. Similar emotions are felt by most saints from time to time. But do not despair, for Jesus said, "I am with you." That promise was a guarantee from Jesus, Himself!

Part three of God's promise centered on God's potential. "For I have many people in this city." Once again Jesus was driving home the point that Paul was not alone. Jesus was there, as were many other servants. That promise assures me that God is at work in a host of people's lives simultaneously. He has an army of believers everywhere. Paul's world at the time was small. He looked at his men and ministry rather than looking at God's kingdom of men. God's kingdom is larger than any preacher's kingdom or any church kingdom. It is larger than any city or any country. This is our Father's world, and He is on His throne. He allows us to have a small part in building His kingdom, but make no mistake: we are not lone rangers in the work of God. Paul needed this reminder, as do most people. Trust His promise, because Jesus said, "I am with you." There is no better comfort than knowing that our Lord is in us and with us. Do you feel discouraged? Do you feel defeated? Do you feel deserted? He is with us! Trust that promise!

To conclude this chapter, permit me to mention some applications we might learn from this promise:

• First, almost everyone feels defeated and discouraged at times. Paul is but one example of that fact.

• Second, do not be afraid to admit your feelings of defeat to God. He already knows about our fears, but He takes pleasure in His servants sharing their thoughts and feelings with Him.

• Finally, God has everything under control. He told Paul that no one was going to hurt him, and "I have many people in this city of which you do not know." When life seems overwhelming, remember: God has everything under control.

CHAPTER 5

GOD WILL NEVER LEAVE YOU

I will never leave you nor forsake you. (Hebrews 13:5)

Life is filled with uncertainties. We live in a world that constantly throws challenges at us from all directions. The COVID-19 pandemic and medical crisis is one example of a way in which life can become unstable. Not since the Spanish flu pandemic of 1918 have medical communities seen so many sick and dying patients. The COVID-19 pandemic death totals may soon surpass historic records for viral pandemic deaths. As of August 2021, this pandemic had caused 4.5 million deaths worldwide and claimed 633 thousand American lives.[11]

I have attempted to console hurting and grieving hearts during the crisis and have been called upon to conduct funerals for victims who were stricken with that horrible virus. I have been infected with the COVID-19 virus, as have many friends and family members.

Struggles for businesses have been enormous, and the dollar costs have been staggering. Non-essential stores were forced to close during much of the 2020 calendar year. People were asked, and sometimes mandated, to wear masks and to socially distance. Children were forced to miss school and receive instruction virtually. Various other tactics were used to slow the spread of the COVID-19 virus.[12] Hospitals were overrun in many parts of the country. The medical community worked tirelessly in efforts to help sick and dying patients. The medical communities were challenged in ways seldom seen. The medical uncertainties seemed to intensify regularly with new variants of the disease.

Another dilemma facing America is the loss of

trust in our institutions. The handling of the war closure in Afghanistan during the 2021 calendar year seemed to exacerbate a feeling of such mistrust. Suspicious questioning of government institutions and their motives of late have sprung up in our culture at large. The war ended with hundreds, or maybe even a thousand, Americans stuck in Afghanistan, which is now controlled by the Taliban.[13] These events have revealed the turbulent domain in which we live. It was reported on one morning news cycle that the American government surrendered to the terrorist Al-Qaeda network, founded by Osama bin Laden. As planes were evacuating civilians from the Kabul airport, a suicide bomber detonated at least one bomb, killing thirteen American soldiers.[14] The president had set an August 31, 2021, deadline for ending all American presence in Afghanistan after twenty years of fighting.

The withdrawal and surrender left many who had fought in the war discouraged and perplexed. Our oldest son was one of many brave soldiers who fought in that bloody conflict. He was wounded and received a Purple Heart for his sacrificial service. Others were not so lucky and were killed, leaving grieving families shaking their heads in disbelief. My son asked, "Dad, what was it for?"

While emotions run high and the future outcome is uncertain, it seems to many that the American interests around the world are in a state of confusion and uncertainty. It also seems that long-respected institutions are now being questioned regarding honesty and transparency.

Another area of suspected instabilities is embedded within various economies. Some Americans are debating the worth of Marxism versus capitalism. That debate is most hotly discussed within the progressive and conservative ideologies. The United States' debt is over $28 trillion, with $5 trillion of that being spent during the 2020 and 2021 calendar years. A bill is before Congress and soon to be voted upon that would add another $5 trillion in governmental spending to the national debt.[15] Economists wonder if the large national debt and spending can be repaid and who will repay it. The economy is certainly debt-weighted and is causing concern and uncertainty in many sectors of the economy.

Families are facing mounting pressures, the likes of which we have seen in decades. Divorce is high, suicide rates are rising, and depression is prevalent in many homes. These issues are present in both the old and young. Some major cities across America have seen spikes in homelessness grow to major proportions. The complexities of family units are causing issues from the workplace to the living room.

With so many problems in our world, what is a Christian to do, and how can one navigate through so many uncertainties? Well, there is good news for the believer. You are not alone, and you do not have to go through these problems in isolation. Our God has promised to "never leave us or forsake us." You can rest on that promise!

Our generation is not the first to endure so many instabilities. The writer of Hebrews gave us some insights into a world that sounds a great deal like ours.

I refer you to Hebrews 13 for a snapshot view of the first century world. In the first verse of that chapter the writer tells believers to "let brotherly love continue." That causes me to think their love for one another was slipping.

Love is a spiritual affection that ought to exist among all believers. Scripture teaches us that the world will know that we are a Christian by our love. As in the first century, twenty-first-century believers are admonished to love one another. Many of the world's problems would be solved if the love of Jesus had a greater hold on believers' lives.

In verse 2, the writer reminds his readers that they sometimes entertain angels unaware. Why was the writer reminding his readers of an angelic presence? I believe he was suggesting that one should live as though an angel of God were standing right beside him. The existence of angels is much debated, and even questioned, in this world. Dr. James R. Gray has written a book, *In the Shadow of the Angels*, in which he describes an angelic moment in his own life. Gray reminds his readers that angels are real and active in our world. The twenty-first-century church would do well to remember that from time to time angels visit people who are not cognizant of their presence. Hebrews reminds us that one's behavior should be so holy it would make the angels proud.

In verse 3 of Hebrews 13, the writer encourages his readers not to forget those who are in prison. Prison is a lonely place, and believers should remember those who are held in bondage. We should pray for them and for their personal needs. I was asked to preach to some inmates in a state prison a couple of years ago. God used that encounter to remind me to pray and be concerned for the souls of prisoners. I witnessed the salvation of several inmates in that prison worship service. People in every generation are cast into prison, and we must not forget about them. The down and out have needs that rival those of the up and out.

In verse 5, the writer moves his readers to focus on the family, reminding them that some marriages were in trouble. Marriage difficulties exist in every century and in every culture. Broken homes abound in every community. Marriages have always been important to God. The home is the oldest institution on earth. It is older than government and older than the church. We should pray for God to protect our marriage and the marriages of others. Marriage partners should strive to move closer to each other and not further apart.

In verse 5, the writer reminds readers never to forget the poor. He also warns the poor to guard against coveting the possessions of those who have more. Be content with what you have, declares the scripture, "for the love of money is the root of all evil" (1 Timothy 6:10).

With so many problems, how should we respond, what are we to do, and where can one go for help? The answer to these questions is contained in a wonderful and rich guarantee given by God. He promised never to leave us or forsake us. That promise can bring stability to a life struggling with the many hardships in this world. If you are sensing your love for those around you slipping and fading, go to God for help, because He is with you and He is for you. When your behavior needs adjusting, let God help you get back on the right path. When you forget to demonstrate the proper attitude toward prisoners, ask God to give you more compassion for them. If you are in bondage to substance abuse and addiction, ask God for deliverance from the control it has over you. When your marriage needs help, God is with you. He is someone to whom you can turn during any crisis. He will never leave you nor forsake you. When you covet, or neglect the poor, God is right there to lean on. He said, "I will never leave you nor forsake you."

Never and nor are used in this verse of promise as a compound negative. Jess Moody said, "I discovered a true nugget when I investigated the semantics of this negative word. It doesn't mean simply a bland never. It is a compounding of five negatives, not each negative added to another, but multiplied by the other. It should read, 'I will never, no not ever, no never leave you, nor forsake you.'"[16] When poverty overtakes you, God is there. When marital problems spring up in your home, God is there. When your behavior is un-becoming a child of God, His Spirit is there to guide you and convict you. When your love for others begins to slip, God is there. When your world turns upside down and seems to be against you, God is there.

A preacher was asked by a couple in his congre-gation to travel to another state and conduct the fu-neral for their son. Their son had been taken to church and Sunday school regularly as a youth, but he had re-belled against the teachings of the church. He had turned to an unnatural and sinful lifestyle. The pastor said there were seventy homosexuals present when he arrived to conduct that funeral. He expressed that he could feel the venom toward him from that audience when he preached from the Bible. He related how God strengthened him and gave him courage to share the gospel in that funeral service.[17] He relied on God's promise to never leave him nor forsake him. That pas-tor explained how the promise of God's presence sustained him in that difficult situation. Just as that pastor experienced God's presence, so too can you in your moments of need. He is with us in this unstable world. He is ready to assist those facing troubling encounters. Even in hours of grief and hurt, God is present. When you encounter situations that are uncomfortable, God will be there. When you go to a funeral, God is with you. When you are facing a host of other types of difficult circumstances, you can trust that the presence of God will accompany you. Why? He promised to never leave us alone.

Verse 6 of Hebrews 13 gives us another great and related promise. He said, "The Lord is my helper, and I will not fear what man shall do unto me." The word "helper" is translated from the Greek word *boethos* and gives the idea that when someone is in trouble, God runs to their aid.

One Sunday our family was returning home from church. Our two young boys were sitting in the back seat. As the car rolled into the carport, our youngest son, Daniel, opened the door almost before the car stopped moving. Daniel always seemed to be in a hurry, while our oldest son, Stephen, seldom got in a hurry. Those were the demeanors God had given them. As Daniel jumped out of the car and closed the door, he screamed with a loud, shrill voice. Immediately I knew something was wrong. He had closed the door on his finger. I quickly got out and ran around to his side of the car. I opened the door to free his finger from the entrapment. His cry told me that he was in pain and needed my help. Likewise, when God hears the cry of His children, He becomes their helper. The word helper carries the idea that He runs to their aid. Therefore, when one is hurting or in trouble, God is ready to be their helper. He will never — no, not ever — leave us alone. His help is unfailing, and his power is unlimited. Our God is a great God, and He has ample ways to meet us at our points of need. Too often we get in trouble and need His help but do not cry out to Him for His help.

A ship was becalmed at sea and stranded off the coast of South America. Almost two weeks went by with no wind. The ship was helpless and could not move. Sailors were about to perish from thirst. Another ship came close enough to hear their frantic cries for help. Upon discovering their need for water, the men on a nearby vessel said, "Let down your buckets."[18] They were directly over a stream of the Amazon River that had fresh, drinkable water.

Likewise, struggling believers sometimes find themselves stranded in troubled situations but do not drop their buckets into the vast supply of God's refreshing streams. He has promised never to leave us nor forsake us. That is a promise from the One who created us and loves us. Drop your bucket today! Cry out to God. He loves you unconditionally and will run to help you in your times of need. He never leaves nor forsakes His children!

To conclude this chapter, allow me to mention some applications that one may draw from this promise:

• First, the Lord is our constant companion and is ready to assist in times of need.

• Second, Jesus is our helper who runs to aid those who cry out for His help.

• Third, during difficult times, trials and tribulations, count on God's encouragement, strength, and partnership.

CHAPTER 6

THE POWER OF HOPE

For I know the plans I have for you, declares the Lord, plans for welfare and not for evil, to give you a future and a hope. (Jeremiah 29:11, ESV)

God has a plan for every believer, and His plan is wrapped in blessings of hope. Those blessings of hope are both temporal and eternal. His promise of hope is penned by various writers throughout Scripture. The words of Jeremiah will be studied as we examine that promise of hope in this chapter. I will opine on the thoughts made by him and other writers throughout the Bible.

Paul and Peter, for example, further developed Jeremiah's wonderful promise of hope. So let's first explore the words of Jeremiah. He declared, "For I know the plans I have for you, declares the Lord, plans to prosper you and not harm you, plans to give you hope and a future" (Jeremiah 29:11, NIV). The framework for this promise is found in the 28th chapter of Jeremiah. It centered around a false promise giving false hope to the people of God. Israel had been defeated and taken captive by the Babylonians. Their brightest and best had been enslaved. Men like Daniel, Shadrach, Meshach, and Abednego had been taken to Babylon as minions and chamberlain servants. The captivity was brought about as the result of Israel's rebellion and disobedience toward God. Jeremiah had told Israel that captivity would come and last for seventy years. However, Hananiah, the son of Azzur, told the people that captivity would come but be short-lived. He guaranteed them that within two years the people of Jerusalem would be back in their land and homes. This prophet gave false hope and contradicted the message sent from God through Jeremiah. Because Hananiah lied to the people and misrepresented God, he was taken off the face of the earth. His death proved that it is dangerous to challenge messages and words sent from God. When Hananiah died, many hearts and hopes were shattered. The people of Jerusalem had bought into the false hope propagated by Hananiah. It is easier for some to believe a lie than accept the truth. People too often believe what they want to believe rather than the hard truth of God. Even while in their rebellious state, God promised to ultimately give them help and not destroy them. God's promise came when Jeremiah guaranteed to them a future and an expectant hope!

Jeremiah's promise revealed the compassionate and loving nature of God. "God is good, a refuge in a time of trouble, and He knows those who trust in Him," declared the prophet Nahum (Nahum 1:7). The God of both heaven and earth promised His children that He would not hurt them, but help them. God's goodness is seen throughout that great promise. God wants the best for us, yet from time to time He is required to exercise chastisement. A spirit of rebellion had entered the heart of Israel, and His chastisement was meant to eradicate that rebellious spirit. These trials came because God loved them, not because He hated them.

When Israel believed the false lies of Hananiah, they further demonstrated their defiance of God. Their unbelief is akin to the easy believe-ism in this generation. When God says repent of sin, some bristle like porcupines and accept the Devil's lies rather than turn from things that are wrong. This generation is guilty of presuming upon God's goodness and believing that a loving God would never allow hardships to come upon them. However, God certainly chastises those He loves. But even in periods of chastisement, He never quits loving, caring for, or nurturing His children. His very nature brings love and hope to rebellious people.

The father of the prodigal son, with open arms, received his rebellious son back home and ordered the servants to bring the ring and the robe and to kill the fatted calf. His display of love for his prodigal mirrors the loving nature that our Lord expresses toward us.

God never gives up on us and keeps loving us even through periods of correction.

The promise of hope and a future was a reminder that God had a plan for Israel that they could not see. He taught them that He was planning good things for them. Hope gave them an expectant confidence that better days would arrive. When God promised them a hope and a future, it was as good as done. He would not change His plan of chastisement, but He would help them get beyond their spirit of rebellion and look for a better day.

You may be living through some hard days brought into your life by bad decisions, rebellion, or even rejection of God's Word. Like the prodigal, you may have wandered into a far country. If that is your story, then there is good news for you: God still loves you and has a plan for your life! He offers hope for your future and help for your present. He wants you to know that He will never harm you and will work situations out for your good and His glory. Regardless of what you are experiencing, never give up on yourself, and never forget that God has a plan and offers you hope.

The Apostle Paul gave further insight into God's promise of hope. He said, "If in this life only we have hope in Christ, we are of all men most miserable" (1 Corinthians 15:19). That verse teaches us that God's hope does not apply only to this temporal world, but also to the eternal world. God's hope for this world is sure, but His hope for the world to come is just as certain.

Our hope in God is an expectation and a confidence that will be revealed through one's life in heaven. If the temporal world was all that one looked forward to, then he would be most miserable. If this life was all there was, then everyone would be discouraged, distressed and without motivation to do good. Our lives would be lived in the sewer of sin. We would live every day with the attitude of "Eat, drink and be merry." The motivation to help others and to be a Good Samaritan would be lost. However, God promised us hope! That hope is sure and secure. Our hope will be lived out in this would, but further hope will be realized in God's eternal world.

The promise of hope is both visible and invisible. Hope is both terrestrial and celestial. It is valuable for the temporal life and secured in eternal life. God has promised a hope that is wrapped up in His unique plan for every Christian. God nurtures His plan in us to prosper us, and not harm us. The hope that God gives us is through His Son, Christ Jesus.

As Edward Mote wrote in his old hymn, "My hope is built on nothing less than Jesus' blood and righteousness. I dare not trust the sweetest frame but wholly lean on Jesus' name. On Christ the solid Rock I stand, all other ground is sinking sand, all other ground is sinking sand."[19]

God sent His Son to be our Savior and Lord. He paid our sin-debt at Calvary, and because of that sacrificial work, He can supply hope to all who believe. Jesus is our best friend and our coming king. He is the One upon whom we lean. He gives confidence for the present and hope for the future. Apart from Jesus, we would have no future or hope, but in Him we have the blessed hope.

God is the most powerful force in the universe, and His power guarantees hope for His children. Biblical hope brings optimism and lofty expectation to those who place their faith in God. It gives the power of belief to the lowly as well as the exalted. Hope develops a reservoir of confidence, because God has promised to help and not hurt. When things seem hopeless and the trials of life are against you, know that you can find peace and safety on your knees. We can cry out to the One who made the promise and who supplies the victory over all our trials and tribulations. The power of hope is strong and comforting. It is like a shield of armor and a refuge from the storm.

Years ago, Parade Magazine printed the story of the self-made millionaire Eugene Lang and how he changed the lives of a sixth-grade class in East Harlem.[20] Mr. Lang had been asked to speak to a group of fifty-nine sixth-graders. What could he say to inspire these students, most of whom would become school dropouts? He wondered how he could get those predominantly Black and Puerto Rican children to even look at him. "Scrapping his notes, he decided to speak to them from his heart. 'Stay in school,' he admonished, 'and I'll help pay the college tuition for every one of you.' At that moment the lives of those students changed. For the first time they had hope. Said one student, 'I had something to look forward to, something waiting on me. It was a golden feeling.'" Nearly ninety percent of that class went on to graduate from high school. Why? They had hope!

What God promises is more awesome than anything a millionaire can offer. God's promise of hope is for security, both in this life and the life to come. He promised to help us and not harm us, prosper us and give us hope, both now and throughout eternity. What a promise!

To conclude this chapter, allow me to mention some applications one may glean from this promise:

• First, God has a plan for each of His children. His plan is to help and not hurt, even though His results are not always clearly seen by the visible eye.

• Second, listen to the right voices and counsel. False hope is sometimes masked through popular personalities.

• Third, quick fixes are not always the answer for the challenges that face us.

CHAPTER 7

WISDOM

If any of you lacks wisdom, let him ask of God, who gives to all liberally and without reproach, and it will be given him. (James 1:5)

There is no greater human quality lacking in this generation than godly wisdom, and there is perhaps no quality less sought after than godly wisdom. A dire need exists for godly wisdom in every Christian's life. Individuals, churches and nations need the wisdom that comes only from our omniscient God. Lack of wisdom can lead to conflict, strife and even war. The Christian church in America could use a revival of wisdom in this dark and sinful post-Christian culture. No one should live without wisdom, because the apostle James declared that if anyone lacks wisdom then he should ask for it and God will give it liberally. The One who has all wisdom has declared that He will give it to you abundantly. That is a great promise for all Christians!

There are three aspects of this wisdom promise that I will mention in this chapter. The first part is the possibility that people, churches and countries are without godly wisdom. The phrase "if one lacks wisdom" reveals a clear possibility that some do lack wisdom. Both churches and countries are made up by a collection of people. While some may possess a measure of godly wisdom, there is certainly no guarantee the whole group possesses wisdom. In this chapter we will examine some ways that our country, some churches, and individuals lack God's wisdom. An absence of wisdom can affect behaviors and thought patterns of the masses.

The second part of the wisdom promise revolves around the process of acquiring that wisdom. James instructed people who lack wisdom to ask God for it.

The asking involves praying, and praying is at the heart of acquiring wisdom. No one can possess God's wisdom unless they fellowship with God first. A huge part of that fellowship comes through their prayer life. When we talk with God, He listens, and His Spirit imparts to us the life of wisdom. The quantity of wisdom one needs is disclosed to God through an effective prayer life. Everyone does not need the same level of wisdom. The Scripture teaches us to pray and to express our wants and needs to the Lord. The disciples asked Jesus to teach them to pray. No one has a right to have God's wisdom if they refuse to pray and express their need to the Heavenly Father.

The third part of the wisdom promise addresses how freely God offers wisdom to those who want it and ask for it. When one desires godly wisdom, he is in fact admitting he does not have enough, and that it comes from God. Adrian Rogers said, "The voice of wisdom is the voice of God."[21] It is my prayer that God will impart to this generation more wisdom than we currently possess.

In 1999, the State Farm Insurance Company rated the most dangerous intersections for accidents in the United States. The winner, for better or worse, was the corner of Belt Line Road and Midway Road in Addison, Texas. There were 263 reported crashes at that intersection in the Dallas suburb. That averages out to about five wrecks per week, not counting the unreported fender-benders.[22] Twenty years later, in 2019, the most dangerous intersection was claimed by a one-mile stretch of road in Benelam, Pennsylvania, and according to the Highway Traffic Safety Administration there were 170 injuries or deaths that occurred at that location.[23]

As people drive down life's road, they sometimes encounter dangerous intersections. These intersections are frequently referred to as forks in the road. There are those moments when a choice to be made can influence the rest of one's life. Decisions to stop or go, turn right or left, go ahead or turn back, can make all the difference. Perhaps right now you are crossing through one of those dangerous intersections of life.

The Bible offers divine resources to help us maneuver through those threatening crossing zones. One such resource is godly wisdom. James addresses that very issue in James 1:5 and suggests that if you are in one of those crossings and lack wisdom, then ask God for it and He will supply it to you abundantly.

So, what is wisdom? Wisdom is far more than knowledge. It is one of those terms that is difficult to capture in totality. The short definition is knowing how to use the knowledge you have. That definition is akin to Warren W. Wiersbe's definition. He said wisdom is "the right use of knowledge," and he went on to say, "All of us know people that are educated fools. They have brilliant academic records but can not make the simplest decisions of life."[24] He illustrated his point by saying "he once met a gifted professor on a seminary campus that was wearing two hats."[25] I can even top Wiersbe's example. Recently, during one of the spikes in COVID-19, I saw an epidemiologist on a news channel wearing and advocating for three masks.[26]

William Barclay had a somewhat different definition of wisdom than Wiersbe. He defined wisdom as
"knowledge turned into action in the decisions and
personal relationships of everyday life."[27] Lehman
Strauss gives a somewhat different definition than
Wiersbe or Barclay. He said, "Wisdom is discernment
and judgment and dexterity in the application of
knowledge already gained, not only in the arts and sci-
ences but also in the scriptures."[28] However, I think the
theologian whose understanding of wisdom best fits
the Apostle James's wisdom promise is given by A.T.
Robertson. Robertson said, "Wisdom is the right use
of one's opportunities in holy living. It is living like
Christ in accord with the will of God."[29] We will follow
Robertson's explanation for wisdom as we talk about
the great promise made in James 1:5.

Almost every sector of society is crying out for
godly wisdom because it is so lacking in our culture
and country. It is absent in ways that even society itself
does not realize. Let me mention several areas that
seem to be almost devoid of wisdom and in using one's

opportunities in holy living. The first one I will mention involves past court decisions. The political and social scenes in America are virtually bankrupt of godly wisdom. I make this argument based on some decisions made by some of the brightest minds in our country. Let me explain. In 1962 the Supreme Court, in *Engel v. Vitale*, ruled it to be unconstitutional for states to compose official prayers and then encourage their recitation. That ruling basically eliminated schools from using the Lord's Prayer and other such recited prayers. The ruling was further strengthened the next year in the *Abington v. Schempp* decision, which in effect took prayer and Bible reading from schools. In 1971, the Supreme Court handed down another ruling in *Lemon v. Kurtzman* that gave a three-pronged test as to whether a statute passes scrutiny under the First Amendment. That ruling strengthened the prohibition for state-supported financial aid to be available to church-related educational institutions. They argued that such aid violated the establishment clause of the U.S. constitution.

Two years later, the Supreme Court, in *Roe v. Wade*, said that a woman had a right to abortion without excessive government restrictions. Since those historic rulings, the court, in *Obergefell v. Hodges*, ruled that men can marry men and women can marry women. The court, in *Stone v. Graham*, ruled that one cannot post the Ten Commandments on walls in public buildings, even if they are paid for with private funding. Thus, over the past sixty years, there seems to have been a cultural revolution that carved biblical thought out of the public square. I submit that these actions were devoid of godly wisdom. The men and women who led these fights may have been endowed with knowledge, but they were short on godly wisdom.

It seems evident that a revival of godly wisdom is much needed across all sectors of society. With the rise of "cancel culture," the elevation of critical race theory, the rewriting of American history, the tearing down of national monuments, the social justice movement, the Me Too movement, the transgender movement, and a wide variety of other movements, society is silently asking, how do we make sense of these changing norms? There are more movements that I can remember in my lifetime, but with almost every movement, society seems to have been weakened, not strengthened. Thus, godly wisdom and biblical thought is sorely lacking in many sectors of modern culture.

Only God can bring us back to normalcy. Only God can heal our land. Only God can supply us with the wisdom needed for such a time as this. Never has there been a greater need for wisdom, and never has there been a better opportunity to practice godly wisdom. A moral crisis always provides a great opportunity for God's people to demonstrate godly wisdom. May more people be heard speaking out and living truth in a world filled with lies.

Sometimes godly wisdom can be found lacking in the local church. An example of this is seen in 1 Corinthians 5:1-2. It was reported to the Apostle Paul that fornication was commonly being committed in that church body. A young man in that church had taken his father's wife and developed a sensual and sexual relationship with her. He was committing open sin with his stepmother. Their sin was being practiced with the church's passive approval. They were puffed up with pride over this sensual relationship rather than mourning over their sinful lifestyle. That type of reaction by church leaders showed a lack of wisdom. There is no record of Matthew 18 being practiced, nor an attempt at spiritual restoration. The church acted as though the behavior was acceptable and appeared to embrace their erroneous behavior. That first-century church attitude can sometimes be seen in the twenty-first-century church. Some modern liberal progressive churches are guilty of embracing fornication and even same-sex unions. That type of behavior shows a lack of godly wisdom by both the church and the guilty parties. Some churches have accepted as normal homosexuality, transgender surgeries, non-married cohabitating partners, and some have even gone so far as to allow homosexual pastors. Social fellowship seems to be elevated above scriptural guidelines. A.T. Robertson believed wisdom was the right use of one's opportunities in holy living. Certainly, both the first- and twenty-first-century churches have periodically been guilty of lacking godly wisdom.

Just as nations and churches fall short in godly wisdom, so can individual Christians. I could offer multiple examples where godly wisdom was lacking in individual Christian lives. However, I will mention only one, due to space and time, and that example is church attendance. Hebrews 10:25 instructs us not to forsake the assembling of ourselves together. For the child of God, church attendance should be as regular as eating. Parents should lead their families to the house of God on the Lord's Day. They should take their children to Sunday school and worship. However, church attendance is declining in almost every denomination in America. Records show that Southern Baptists, of which I am a member, lost a million people in 2019 — and that was pre-pandemic. Livestream, television and radio have replaced live worship for many believers. Children that have little or no moral training in the public schools are absent from missions, moral and Christian education in churches. The spiritual life of the family is inept in many homes. If families are not regularly engaged in worship and Christian training, then obviously that is an unwise routine.

Should I or shouldn't I go to church? Should I or shouldn't I require my children to attend church? Do I read and teach the Bible stories to my children? Do I accept the guidelines and movements that society is promoting? Is the Bible really true? Should I or shouldn't I follow its commandments. Is God real? Is there life after death, and should I help evangelize others? These are only some of the issues that are asked in this post-Christian America. Thus, all Christians need wisdom that only God can give. Again, it is evident that Christians need a revival of godly wisdom.

The Apostle James stresses that when wisdom is lacking, prayer is the vehicle by which one should secure such wisdom. No one is wise who refuses to pray, but those who do pray can receive wisdom. God teaches us how to flesh out the Christian life. He gives us insight to make personal decisions, cast votes and be a good church member. He helps us see when we are wrong and encourages us to continue when we are right. So if your life is devoid of godly wisdom, then pray! Listen for the voice of God, because the voice of God is the voice of wisdom.

The conditions in this generation tell us that a revival of prayer and wisdom is needed. Medical and financial issues should reveal to us that our world is devoid of the insight needed to solve current emergencies. Almost every sector of society is crying out for godly wisdom in ways that even society itself does not realize. The political and social scenes in America are empty of godly wisdom. As mentioned earlier, the COVID-19 pandemic, according to the Centers for Disease Control and Prevention, has claimed approximately 800,000 American lives despite masks, medicines, vaccines, and the spending of billions of dollars for prevention. Homes and families have been shattered. Grieving loved ones are still asking how such a thing could happen to a society that has the best science and medicines ever recorded. Hospitals have been overrun, doctors and nurses have been over-worked, and people are still dying. The spirit of this age is one of discouragement and, in some cases, even depression.

The national debt has skyrocketed to over $28 trillion, and another $4.5 trillion of spending is being proposed to Congress by the democratic-controlled White House.[30] This debt level has more than tripled over the last two decades. As government continues to grow the debt, government expansion has grown, as well. The governmental intrusion into the lives of normal citizens has caused conflict and division. With attempts to limit both the first and second amend-ments, social conflict is at a generational high. Shoot-ings have increased, murder from abortions keep ris-ing, and society continues to reel in the debt. These and many other issues have caused conflict and stress throughout many parts of this country.

Some think that education and science will solve the problems. The premium of education is in such demand that the tuition rates keep rising. Social problems are great, and many have turned to the scientist and psychologist to fix the problems. Education has made so many advances, yet problems seem to get worse with each passing generation. The issues facing this age cannot and will not be solved with education. Lehman Strauss said, "We have never had more college graduates, and never more educated ignorance."[31] The world's problems will never be solved apart from godly wisdom. Only the Creator of His world knows how to solve the problems in His world. Neither education, nor money, nor politics will solve the mountains of problems this world faces, but Jesus can. I contend that this world needs a revival of godly wisdom.

God is a generous friend. He delights in giving His people the ability to apply their knowledge in the right ways. He longs to help believers make right choices. He yearns to help us make it through the dangerous intersections of life. If you lack wisdom, then ask God, and He will give it to you generously. Thus, one of our constant priorities should be to offer prayers for both ourselves and for those who lead us. Ask God to give our governmental leaders, church leaders, and family leaders godly wisdom. Pray for God to give our educators and youth leaders wisdom. Above all, pray for a revival of wisdom all over the world.

God promised to give anyone wisdom who would ask Him for it. We all need God's help and healing. We all need God's protection in our dangerous intersections. We all need godly wisdom! God promised it to anyone who would ask for it!

To conclude this chapter, permit me to mention some applications that can be learned from this promise:

• First, wisdom is the right use of knowledge in the opportunities one is given for holy living.

• Second, godly wisdom is at war with worldly wisdom.

• Finally, there is a great need for a revival of godly wisdom, and if one is to have such wisdom then it must start with prayer.

CHAPTER 8

EVANGELISM
AND PREACHING

And he said unto them, "Follow me and I will make you fishers of men." (Matthew 4:19)

And He said to them, "Go into all the world and preach the gospel to every creature." (Mark 16:15)

So shall my word that goeth forth out of my mouth; it shall not return unto me void, but it shall accomplish that which I please, and it shall prosper in the thing whereto I sent it. (Isaiah 55:11)

Evangelism and church growth are both a command and a promise. Jesus commanded His disciples to go into all the world and preach the gospel, baptizing them in the name of the Father, Son and Holy Spirit. He then promised to be with them till the end of the age. He taught His church to major on preaching as a tool to win the lost. The Apostle Paul asked, "How shall they hear without a preacher? And how shall they preach except they be sent?" (Romans 10:14-15). God was instructing His followers that preaching and evangelism are not just the responsibility of the preacher. Preaching the gospel to the world should not be a one-man operation. It should be a church-wide collective mission. The church body should be all-in on preaching, evangelism and disciple-making.

Jesus gave multiple supportive statements about evangelism and preaching. For example, He said, in Matthew 24:35, "Heaven and earth will pass away but my word will never pass away." Isaiah shares a similar promise when he said, in Isaiah 55:11, "So shall my word be that goes forth from my mouth; it shall not return to me void but it will accomplish what I please."

Thus, preaching and reaping are both a command and a promise. The command says "Go tell" about Jesus and share the gospel, and the promise is that God will use our voices as an extension of His voice to win the lost.

I earned my doctor of ministry degree, in church growth, at Southeastern Baptist Theological Seminary. I took all the evangelism classes that were offered. My favorite professor was Dr. Delos Miles, who had previously served as the evangelism director for the South Carolina Baptist Convention. Dr. Miles would often refer to his own writings while teaching those classes. He had penned the book, *Church Growth: A Mighty River*. I learned from Dr. Miles that church growth is as old as the church.[32] Jesus-modeled evangelism and preaching have headwaters that run in all directions. There are large tributaries and small streams, and all of them are important to God. He will use any person, or groups of people, who will share His words and make disciples. So if preaching and evangelism are important to God, and they are, then what type of preaching is best utilized for evangelism? While all Bible preaching is honored by God, Jesus had a distinct style. It is what I call the "Jesus model" of preaching. Now remember: All people can trust God's promises, and Jesus said, "Follow me, and I will make you fishers of men." Furthermore, God promised that His words would never pass away. So, we must never be ashamed to use God's Word and, when opportunities allow, use them to fish for the souls of men. His words and methods will produce fruit and will never return to Him void. For that reason, I have attempted to follow the Jesus model as I understand it. The following principles were modeled when Jesus, Himself, was preaching.

Jesus is both the message and messenger of salvation. No one else can lay hold to that fact. He is the center and circumference of the Bible. He is the Promised One of the Old Testament and the Holy One of the New Testament. Every called preacher is a messenger of the gospel, but only Jesus is the gospel. Mark 1:14-15 tell us that Jesus "came preaching the gospel of the kingdom of God, and saying, 'The time is fulfilled, and the kingdom of God is at hand: repent and believe the gospel.'" He sent the twelve out to preach, and said, in Luke 19:10, that "the Son of man has come to seek and to save those which are lost." Thus, the priority of Jesus' ministry was preaching and calling sinners to repentance. He gives this model to all gospel preachers as a roadmap to follow. That model was used by those He sent out and should be used by the ones trained to be sent out in all generations.

Bold evangelistic preaching is needed in every age, and believers should pray for fiery pulpits, aflame with the message and model of Jesus. Preachers exalt Jesus through preaching and would be wise to follow His model while expounding God's Word. God's Word is what every preacher possesses to proclaim. There-fore, the Jesus preaching model is proclamational. Je-sus was "the Herald from heaven," and He never lost sight of Who sent him and what His mission was. His proclamation came on the heels of John the Baptist's imprisonment for bold preaching. This tells me that

Jesus was no wimp. Even on the heels of John's imprisonment, He boldly proclaimed that people should "come." His message was a call to leave sin and self and follow the Savior. He asked people to leave their sinful lifestyles and live lives of holiness.

No one can be saved and remain as they are. Billy Graham once said, "We are dangerously close to saying to the prodigal that you do not have to return to the father and home, we will make you comfortable in the pig pen."[33] The Jesus model of preaching proclaims that people must repent. They must turn to the new life offered in Christ Jesus. Good proclamation calls people to unequivocally leave sin and self and come to the Savior.

The Jesus model of preaching is invitational. It is illogical to preach without an invitation or appeal. Virtually every sermon should be followed by an invitation. Jesus used words like "come," "follow me" and "believe" to give a call for sinners to be saved. If Jesus gave his hearers an invitation to "come," to "follow," then so should preachers in every age. Churches will not grow and the kingdom will not expand if preachers do not give invitations.

There is power in an invitation. Church Trainer Group gives statistics about people being invited to church and states that 83 percent of attendees come because they are invited.[34] They state that 6-8 percent walk in by their own initiative, and 2-3 percent come because they like a program, 8-10 percent come because they like the pastor, and 70-85 percent come because they are invited by a friend or relative. The Billy Graham Evangelistic Association conducted a survey and found that unchurched people would come to church if invited by a relative or friend.[35] These statistics reveal the power in an invitation. Thus, does it not make sense that a pastor or preacher should use the power of an invitation to urge people to "come" to the Savior? People should be given an opportunity to do something with the sermon, through the drawing of the Holy Spirit. The preacher proclaims Jesus, and the Spirit draws people to repent. An invitation is needed to allow the process of conviction and conversion to take place. Jesus used the term "come" often in His appeal to sinners, because there is power in an invitation.

Too often, preachers stop short of asking people to do something with the sermon. Jesus gave invitations — an appeal for listeners to do something with His sermons and the lessons they had heard. He wanted them to repent and come into fellowship with His Father.

The Jesus model of preaching is expectational. Jesus never gave a sermon or invitation without expecting a response. He demanded repentance in Mark 1:14. He asked people to change their mind about sin, and, in Mark 1:15, He followed up His appeal for repentance by asking them to "believe." The word "believe" is a word of action, which suggests that repentance and faith are inseparable. Faith is the foundation upon which repentance rests. When Jesus gave invitations, it was with the expectation that His hearers would respond to His appeal. His appeal was sometimes met with a no, as with the rich young ruler, and sometimes with a yes, as with Zacchaeus. Whether the response was negative or positive, Jesus was consistent in asking and expecting a response to His invitations. He gave invitations with an expectant heart, and every gospel preacher should do the same. His model of expectation with anticipation happened regularly!

The Jesus model of preaching is developmental. Jesus said, "I will make you fishers of men" (Matthew 4:19). Soul-winners are made, not born. Every sermon should be laced with instructions containing eternal significance. Jesus took common, ordinary working people and made them into soul-winners who fished for the souls of men. He developed them into a force that changed the world.

When a preacher stands to deliver a sermon, he should appeal not only for lost men to be saved, but also for saved men to grow and develop. The greatest platform in every church is not the teaching lectern, it is the pulpit. The man of God should always go there with a sermon that has been well prepared and prayed over, with the goal of helping his hearers develop into a spiritual reproductive soul-winning army. He needs both to appeal to the lost and to develop the saved.

After I preached one Sunday, a young lady in our congregation became burdened over her lost dad, who lived in another state. She asked me how she could win him to Jesus. I told her about a soul-winning class that was soon to begin. She joined that class and studied her "Continued Witnessing Training" manual diligently. The class prayed both for her to witness and for her dad to be saved. The time came for her and her military husband to travel home to another state. She witnessed to her dad with nervousness in her heart. No one could have been more tense than that young lady, but through faith she believed God would save her lost dad. Words do not allow me to express the depth of joy I felt when my she called to say, "Preacher Wayne, he got saved! He got saved!" I could hear excitement amidst her sniffling and tears. Her dad had moved from death to life, and she was rejoicing over his salvation. That experience taught me the value of developing soul-winners. Good preaching is both evangelistic and developmental. The Jesus preaching model attempts to do both.

The Jesus model of preaching is eternal. Only heaven can know the eternal benefits of preaching. Jesus constantly caused men to think about eternal things rather than to dwell on temporal things. People normally tend to focus on earthly things, such as "Which job can I acquire?" or "How much money can I make?" or "Which house can I afford?" or "Which team will I support?" Temporal thoughts often center on the latest fashion and on human popularity. Jesus, on the other hand, invariably caused people to think about heaven and hell, life and death. He caused potential followers to count the cost of salvation and discipleship. The rich young ruler refused to follow Jesus because he was very wealthy and was forced to choose between material things and heavenly things. The Jesus model of preaching always leads men to the eternal rather than the temporal.

Dwight L. Moody professed that the greatest mistake he made in his ministry was sending some people home one Sunday without giving an invitation. In October 1871, Moody told his congregation to go home and think about the message and come back the next Sunday ready to make a decision for Christ. Before they came together again, a fire started in Patrick O'Leary's barn. The fire spread throughout the area, leaving 300 people dead and more than 100,000 people homeless. Moody explained that, never again would he dare give his audience a week to think about their salvation. He said, "I have never seen that congregation since .... I would rather have my right hand cut off than to give an audience a week now to decide what to do with Jesus."[36]

Failure to give an invitation is to deviate from the Jesus preaching model. He declared that He came to seek and to save those who were lost. His model for accomplishing His task included at least five components. Those components were proclamation, invitation, expectation, developmental, and eternal. Preachers in every age would be wise to follow the Jesus model as their preaching model.

When the preacher and people unite to do evangelism, God has promised to use it to make disciples and grow His church.

To conclude this chapter, allow me to offer some applications that one can take away from this promise:

• First, Jesus is the model that all preachers should follow in their proclamation. He is the only one who can lay claim to being both the message and messenger.

• Second, no sermon is complete without an invitation. Failure to give an invitation is to deviate from the Jesus preaching model.

• Third, preaching was used by Jesus to both win the lost and develop the saved.

CHAPTER 9

REWARD AND CROWN

I have fought the good fight, I have finished the race, I have kept the faith. Finally, there is laid up for me the crown of righteousness, which the Lord, the righteous Judge, will give to me on that Day, and not to me only but also to all who have loved His appearing. (2 Timothy 4:7-8)

The Apostle Paul's life was nearing an end. It is reported he was executed around AD 67 in Rome by the Caesar, just a short while after penning the great promise found in 2 Timothy 4:7-8.[37] He believed his reward was waiting for him in heaven and that he would receive it immediately after death. Paul wrote that the heavenly rewards were not for him only, but for all those who love the Lord's appearing. He was shining a light on the eternal fellowship with God revealed through this great promise.

It is a celebration time when a believer is taken to his heavenly home. It brings with it a reunion with friends, family and, greatest of all, Jesus. Christians will receive in heaven their rewards for services rendered on earth. Their citizenship will give them standing in the city of God. Heaven's rewards are reserved for those who love the Lord's appearing and are not limited to preachers like Paul. They will be given out to virtually every saint of God.

Physical death is not something people wish for every day. The pains and hurts that lead to death are not pleasant. However, our rewards are just beyond the grave and will certainly be satisfying. They will bring rejoicing to the saints of God and cause celebration over all of heaven. Paul was looking beyond the grave when he described those coming events. In these next few pages, we will examine the events that led to Paul's peace and God's promise.

Paul was declaring that he would not turn back, even if given the opportunity. Heaven was before him, and he was ready to press on and cross the finish line. He was ready to complete his race. He had come this far by faith, leaning on the Lord. Heaven was within sight and his race was nearly over. His attitude and testimony remind me of a song, "We've Come This Far by Faith," written by Albert Goodson.[38] Goodson was in Chicago, lonely and discouraged. Having left his family, friends, and church acquaintances back in Los Angeles, he took a new job in Chicago. It was a new and strange city to him, and he found himself being tempted to go back. Goodson, a great pianist, was given the opportunity to play someone else's instrument, and began to play a new tune, and on that piano he put together a song that expressed his faith and his need to lean upon the Lord.

Paul was nearing the end of his trail. He was about to take his journey to the other side, and he summed up his testimony by saying, "I have fought the good fight, I have finished my race, I have kept the

faith. There is laid up for me the crown of righteousness, which the Lord, the righteous judge, will
give me on that Day, and not to me only but also to all
those who have loved his appearing." While writing
those words at the end of his life's journey, he found
himself reflecting on some of the Christian acquaintances with whom he had labored. Some of those
memories were good, and some not so good. However,
God gave him grace for the good and the bad.

Let me mention several acquaintances who were
on his mind as he sat in his prison cell. I believe most
people tend to have such reflective moments. Taking a
mental inventory about meaning, accomplishments
and relationships is a normal thing for a person nearing the end of his life. Certainly, Paul was in deep
thought, and with pen in hand, he began to write
about his memories of ministry friends and enemies.
His end-of-life reflections were therapeutic.

On one occasion, I made a visit to a church
member who had been told by his doctor that he had
only days to live. My goal was to offer encouragement

to him, but as with many such visits, I was the one who received the encouragement. I sat in that man's home and said, "Ben, I hear that the doctor has told you that you have a short time left, barring a miracle from God." He affirmed that in fact he had received that news and asked if I would preach his funeral. I said, "It will be an honor to do that, and when I preach your funeral, is there anything you want me to say?" He looked at me with a smile on his face and said, "Preacher, you tell them that my God is real."

The Apostle Paul was having one of those "My God is real" moments when he began to jot down some memories about his acquaintances. One such acquaintance was a man named Demas, who had left Paul and the work of God and made his journey to Thessalonica. His love for the world became greater than his love for God and ministry. Demas is mentioned three times in Scripture. His résumé is a picture of a defeated servant. The first reference to that defeated man was given in the 24th verse of Philemon when he was called "Demas, my fellow laborer." He was at his post, faithfully serving alongside the Apostle Paul. He is described as having his hands to the plow, enthusiastically doing missions and evangelism. He was on the firing line for God. However, his second reference was in Colossians 4:14. In that text he was simply referred to as Demas. The picture seems to suggest that the fires had cooled, and he was not as excited about doing the work of the church. Too many Christians do work by rote rather that giving an enthusiastic effort to God. The third and final time Demas is referenced is 2 Timothy 4:10, when Paul remembers and reports that Demas was AWOL (absent without leave). He had allowed the things of this world and the desire for money to lure him away from his assigned post. Thus, Paul was in his cell reflecting with sadness about some who had left the work of the Lord. Demas came to his mind and was described as a defeated Christian. Demas had departed from the work of the Lord.

Another memory Paul wrestled with during his last hours was his recollection of Alexander. He was described as a dangerous man, and Paul said about

him, "He has done me much harm" (2 Timothy 4:14).
Little is known about Alexander except that he was an
enemy of the cross. He stood against the work Paul
was attempting to do for God. Could it be that this
Alexander was the one who was at the cross when Jesus was crucified? Simon of Cyrene, who carried the
cross of Jesus to the hill called Golgotha, had two sons.
One was named Alexander (Mark 15:21) and the other
one was named Rufus. Rufus is referenced as a faithful
servant in Romans 16:13. Could it be that this Alexander was the son of that Roman soldier who carried the
cross of the Jesus? Others think the Alexander mentioned here by Paul is the coppersmith in 1 Timothy
1:19-20. Whoever this man named Alexander was, he
was no friend to Paul, nor to the church. In Paul's final
hours of life, he recalled the harm that had befallen
him by the hands of Alexander. He was a dangerous
man. Perhaps each of us can recall some people in life
who have caused us harm. My takeaway from this story is that Paul did not attempt retribution, but rather
turned Alexander over to the Lord. He said, "The Lord

reward him according to his works." That model and example should lend wisdom to people in all generations. We would fare better by allowing the Lord to deal with our enemies rather than taking matters into our own hands.

Another memory that brought joy to Paul's heart was his recollection of Luke. Luke was dependable. He was with Paul as they planted churches and won people to Christ. He was a writer and doctor who seldom allowed a spotlight to shine upon himself. He was with Paul in Rome as an encourager when the angel of death stood at Paul's door. Paul wrote, "Luke is with me" (2 Timothy 4:11). This is a picture of dependability. Luke was portrayed as a friend and ministry associate who was faithful and dependable to the end.

I am grateful for dependable men whom God puts in our paths along life's way. One such church acquaintance came my way in my first pastorate. A financial issue arose that seemingly was going to cause a church building program to go up in smoke. I went to seek counsel from one of the deacons on a rainy day. He was a farmer, and on that day, it was too wet to plow or work in the fields. When I arrived at his house, he was sitting on his back porch, watching the rain fall. I sat down in a rocker beside him and said, "Clyde, it looks as though the building program is in trouble. The problem that has arisen could blow it up." That wise old deacon, who never quit rocking, said, "Preacher, do you believe that God led you to lead us to build that building?" I said, "Yes, with all my heart, I believe that." Clyde said, "Then what has changed?" I left there encouraged, knowing what I needed to do. That building was built (and debt-free, I might add). Clyde was a dependable and calming voice to this young preacher. I will forever be indebted to men like Clyde Powell, who were used by God to give counsel and encouragement during times of adversity.

Paul reflected upon Luke's faithfulness and dependability. His faithfulness brought happy memories to Paul during his last hours of life. Be grateful when God allows faithful saints to bless your life.

Next, as Paul began to do some self-reflection, he said, "The Lord stood with me" (2 Timothy 4:17). God delivered Paul from all sorts of danger — from prison in Philippi and from mobs in various cities. God protected him when a contract was placed on his life and when evil men covenanted together to kill the old preacher. God showed up as his refuge in times of need, and Paul acknowledged that he was a delivered man.

However, Paul's greatest and best memories were about the Divine Man, Jesus. Paul gave credit to the one who saved him, kept him, protected him and delivered him. That man was Jesus, his constant companion. His name is above every name. He possesses a divine name and a divine nature: "He made him who knew no sin to become sin for us that we might become the righteousness of God in Him" (2 Corinthians 5:21). Thus, the old preacher was not feeling sorry for himself, but rather rejoicing, knowing that his home-going was getting near.

Paul turns to the statement of promise: "Finally,

there is laid up for me a crown of righteousness, which the Lord, the righteous Judge, will give me on that day, and not to me only but also to all those who have loved His appearing." That promise is for every Christian. The appearing of the Lord may come at death, or it may be at the rapture. Whenever it occurs, there will be a crown waiting for each saint of God in heaven. That promise of a reward and crown is as sure as breathing. So, in closing this chapter about the promise of a reward and crown, I take you back to the song by Albert Goodson that so well describes so many saints of God: "Oh, we've come this far by faith, leaning on the Lord, trusting in His holy Word. He's never failed me."

To conclude this chapter, permit me to mention some applications one might draw from this promise:

• First, men do sometimes disappoint you. Certainly Demas, Alexander and others had disappointed Paul.

• Second, some people had done Paul harm. Yet he did not seek retribution. He left the rewarding of judgment to the Lord and trusted God to handle the matter justly.

• Finally, it is important to keep our eyes focused on the main things. Heaven was in sight, and finishing the race was more important than self-gratification.

Chapter 10

Raptured

And while they looked steadfastly toward heaven as he went up, behold, two men stood by them in white apparel; which also said, ye men of Galilee, why stand ye here gazing up into heaven? This same Jesus, which is taken up from you into heaven, shall so come in like manner as ye have seen Him go into heaven. (Acts 1:10-11)

Jesus is coming again! That promise is one of the greatest treasures given to a child of God. That promise, like a rainbow in the sky, encourages preachers to believe it and preach about it, churches to expect it, and Christians to watch for it. The promise of the second coming of Jesus brings great hope to all the ages. The One who was arrested, beaten, spat upon, cursed, crucified, buried and risen, stood upon the Mount of Olives and ascended back to heaven. His mission on earth was completed, and He went to reoccupy His place at the right hand of His Father's throne in heaven. He had been on earth doing the will of His Father for thirty-three years. His work was now finished, Calvary was conquered, and salvation was provided. The sin-debt had been paid! It was time for Jesus to return to His heavenly home and prepare a place for the saints of God.

As He ascended, one of the greatest promises in Scripture was voiced to His disciples by the angel of God: "Now when He had spoken these things, while they watched, He was taken up, and a cloud received Him out of their sight. And while they looked steadfastly toward heaven as He went up, behold, two men stood by them in white apparel, who also said, 'Men of Galilee, why do you stand gazing into heaven? This same Jesus, who was taken from you into heaven, will so come in like manner as you saw Him go into heaven'" (Acts 1:9-11).

The Apostle Paul said, when speaking about the second coming, said, "We shall not all sleep, but we shall all be changed, in a moment, in a twinkling of an eye, at the last trump: for the trumpet shall sound, and the dead shall be raised incorruptible, and we shall be changed" (1 Corinthians 15:51-52). Later, he said, "For the Lord himself shall descend from heaven with a shout, with the voice of the archangel, and with the trump of God ... then we which are alive and remain shall be caught up together with them in the clouds, to meet the Lord in the air: and so shall we ever be with the Lord" (1 Thessalonians 4:16-17).

The rapture is what is being referred to when Scripture speaks about being raised or caught up. Although the word "rapture" is not used in the Bible, the event is referred to repeatedly. The technical moment of the second coming is when Jesus sets foot on earth after the seven years of tribulation. The catching up of believers will happen just before the tribulation. This eschatological view believes that the rapture will trigger a seven-year tribulation period on earth for those who were not saved and left behind. That eschatological view also believes that during the seven-year tribulation period, the antichrist will rule the world and deceive the left-behind human race. At the end of the tribulation, Jesus will return, riding a white horse, and then He will set up His reign on earth where He will rule and reign from Jerusalem for 1,000 years (Revelation 19:11-19).

Just know that when I refer to the second coming, I am referring to the "catching up of believers" into heaven. God Himself made that promise, and there are several aspects to Jesus' second coming promise I want to mention.

The promise of a second coming of Jesus is just as trustworthy and dependable as God's promise to send a messiah. The trustworthiness of that promise is rooted in faith. We should take God at His word. We should believe that Jesus is coming again, just as much as we believe the sun is going to rise tomorrow. Believing the promise of the second coming enriches one's faith and builds one's confidence in God. Jesus made that proclamation to His disciples but intended it for all those who would follow Him by faith. Jesus said, "I will come again, and receive you unto myself, that where I am, there ye may be also" (John 14:36).

John Knox was a great Scottish preacher of another generation. His early ministerial career was in and around Geneva, Switzerland. He left Geneva and went to southern Europe to minister. The people missed him so much that there was a campaign for his return to Geneva. He accepted their request to return and began making arrangements. When word spread about his planned return, the news spread quickly through the streets of the city. It was reported that people in passing would ask, "Have you heard? Knox is coming! Knox is coming." The people of Geneva were so excited that they proclaimed it throughout the city.[39]

Certainly Knox was loved and respected. He was a great leader and preacher. But John Knox, compared to Jesus, was minuscule in size. Jesus is the Lord of Lords and the King of Kings. He is Savior, Sustainer,

Provider and, one day, Coming King. The excitement about Knox should pale in comparison to news that Jesus is coming. The church should shout in every city, "Jesus is coming!" We should ask everywhere, "Have you heard that Jesus is coming?" Time and space are inadequate for this writer to talk about the complete details regarding the return of Jesus. However, I will mention a few aspects of His coming in hopes that it will build your faith. May His promised return so grip the hearts of the saved that they will go throughout the cities and countryside asking, "Have you heard? Jesus is coming!"

God gave not only proclamation of His coming, but also instructions regarding His coming. Jesus said, "Watch therefore, for you do not know what hour your Lord is coming" (Matthew 24:42). The English word "watch" is translated from a Greek word meaning, "stay awake and be alert."[40] This mandate is wrapped in mystery, because no one knows just when the rapture will occur. But trust His promise: It will happen. Jesus is coming, and that is surer than life, itself.

A group of fishermen was arriving on shore when one of the men picked up a pair of binoculars and said, "Hey Greg, I see your wife, Susie. Bill, I see your wife, Kate. Randy, I spot Michelle in the distance." Richard, taking offense that his wife was not called out, grabbed the binoculars, but he did not see his wife, Amy, standing on the dock. Feeling a little hurt, Richard jumped into his truck and started home. When he walked into the house, his wife shouted, "Welcome home! I've been waiting for you." Richard despondently replied, "Yes, you were waiting, but the other men's wives were watching for them."[41]

There is a big difference between waiting and watching. Jesus said, "Watch," and the idea is that the church should anxiously, consistently and eagerly watch for His coming. It is a great privilege to watch for the return of Jesus.

Another aspect of His coming is the evacuation that is described. When God catches away His bride, the church, it will be done orderly and systematically. God is not the author of confusion, and when He does something, He does it decently and with order. Scripture tells us that the second coming will be sudden. (Remember, Paul declared that in a moment and in the twinkling of an eye, the trump will sound, and the church will be gone.) The systematic approach describes the orderliness of the event. The dead will rise first, and then those who remain will be caught up to be with the Lord in the sky.

The precision that God uses to usher His church home reflects the character of God. The church will be physically elevated to heaven. It will occur flawlessly and methodically. God is not the author of confusion. While there may be bewilderment and uncertainty on earth after that event takes place, make no mistake: God has flawlessly planned the details about getting His bride home. He is coming for her in the clouds. What a promise!

Not only does Jesus instruct us about His elevation and expectations, but He also discloses the elation that His bride will relish. She will take joy in the marriage. The church will leave a sin-cursed, confused and chaotic world behind. The dirt and filth of this world will be replaced by clean streets of gold and crystal streams of water. Pearls will be abundant, and the gates of the city of God will be made with them.

The bride of Christ will leave behind all sorts of sufferings and will arrive in a place where there will be no pain, no tears, no death and no sorrows. She will live in mansions made by her groom. She will sing hallelujah to the Lamb! What a place! What a joy! What a promise!

Added to all this is the future reunion and rejoicing among the saints. There will be fellowship with the ones on whose shoulders we have stood while serving our Lord on earth. Friends, be glad! Jesus is coming again! Jesus never fails! Because of His fellowship with us, His principles around us, and His favor toward us, I have learned to trust Him. Therefore, I confess before the world that I trust His promise and I believe Jesus is coming again!

To conclude this chapter, permit me to offer some applications one can learn from this promise:

- First, Jesus is coming soon!

- Second, watch! There is a huge difference between waiting and watching.

- Finally, the second coming will be sudden, orderly, and exciting. It will happen in a moment and in the blink of an eye, when the last trumpet is blown.

Conclusion

The basis for *Trust God's Promises* grew out of personal experiences in my own faith. I was saved in May of 1967, and since that time God has proven Himself faithful to me and my family. Time and again, I have gotten on my knees asking God to produce the fruit of His promises in me. Never have I been disappointed! My requests were not always granted in the way I imagined, but God was always faithful in keeping His promises. His promises produce events, activities, and mysteries that no mortal person can fathom. God prevents heartaches that are as important as His visible blessings upon us. A verse that reveals that truth is Malachi 3:11. He stated that God would rebuke the devourer for our sakes, and that promise assures us that we enjoy both His visible blessings as well as His unseen protections.

Throughout life's journey, I have discovered that God loves me unconditionally, protects me forcibly, and guides me continually. God never fails! "Simply trusting every day, trusting through a stormy way; even when my faith is small, Trusting Jesus, that is all. Trusting as the moments fly, Trusting as the days go by; Trusting Him whate'er befalls, Trusting Jesus, that is all."[42]

Through the good times and bad, I have learned to trust God's promises. All of them are true, valid, available, and trustworthy to anyone who claims them by faith. The ten promises written about in this project are but a few of the pledges made to us by our God. These ten chapters about God's promises are a feeble attempt to remind the reader that promises made by God are promises kept. Faithful is our Creator and Loving Lord. Jesus is a friend who sticks closer than a brother, and He wants to walk with us through the intersections of life. Like the rainbow in the sky, this book is an attempt to remind you of the trustworthiness and reliability of God. May we learn daily to *Trust God's Promises!*

Acknowledgments:

I would like to thank several people who contributed to this writing project:

• Anita Dickard, for proofreading, looking up sources for this book, and any other needs that I asked of her. She is the best.

• Sherry Spence and Ann Mullikin, for taking the beautiful pictures of a rainbow in the sky over Easley, South Carolina.

• The ten members of the Calumet Baptist Church, Liberty, South Carolina, who read a chapter each and gave feedback about errors and ideas they found in their chapter.

• The senior adult group from Eastside Baptist, Liberty, South Carolina, my first Trust God's Promises study group while on a senior adult retreat.

• Dr. Evans Whitaker, for writing the foreword to this book. Dr. Whitaker is president of Anderson University, my alma mater.

• Dr. Joe Hopkins, president of Campbellsville

University, Mrs. Julie Cannon, author and public school guidance counselor, and Dr. Gary Hollingsworth, executive director-treasurer of the South Carolina Baptist Convention, for writing endorsements for this book. These people are some of the greatest Christians friends that I have on earth.

• The staff of the Baptist Courier, for their help in publishing this book.

To all these wonderful people, I say thanks.

Notes

1 *Abraham Lincoln: The Man and His Faith*. George Owen. "President Lincoln's Promise." Ministry 127.com.

2 The trial of Martin Luther: an account." www.famous-trials.com.

3 "Christmas-Missing the point." Preaching.com.

4 Air and space. Si. Edu and loc.gov *Part of Words and Deeds in American History: Selected Documents Celebrating the Manuscript Division's First 100 years (87).*

5 "John 3:16 and the Homeless Boy." Friday Study Ministries. www.fridaystudy.org.

6 "Love, N. and V." *The Random House Dictionary of the English Language*, College Edition, New York, 1968.

7 Woolston, Clare Herbert. "Jesus Loves the Little Children." George F. Root, 1861.

8 "Your Faces Gives it Away." In Other Words. Contributed by Guy McGraw on March 12, 2009. www.Sermoncentral.com.

9 "Love, N. and V., ibid.

10 Lehman, Frederick M. "The Love of God." Public domain.

11 "CDC COVID Tracker," covid.cdc.gov.

12 "What you Need to Know about Variants." Nov.1, 2021. www.cdc.gov/variants.

13 Fox News.

14 Risch, Senator Jim (R-Idaho). Who is responsible for the Afghanistan withdrawal debacle? October 26, 2021. Risch.senator.gov.

15 "So…just how concerned should we be about America's $28 Trillion debt?" March 1, 2021. www.wlbt.com.

[16] Moody, Jess. "The Most Encouraging Verse in the Bible." Allen, R. Earl and Gregory, Joel, compilers. *Southern Baptist Preaching Today.* Nashville, Tennessee: Broadman Press, 1987, p. 259.

[17] Ibid. p. 261.

[18] "Need Not Go On With Thirst." Christian Cheong. Sermoncentral.com.

[19] "My Hope Is Built on Nothing Less," Mote, Edward. Public domain.

[20] Schlaepfer, René. "The Effect of Hope." *The Hope Experience, 50 Days of Hope,* Day 26. www.hopeexperience.com.

[21] Rogers, Adrian. "Wisdom's Final Call." www.sermoncentral.com.

[22] "State Farm names most dangerous intersections." Americancityandcounty.com. 5th July 2001.

[23] Turnbell, Michael. "Pines Intersection Ranks 1st in crashes."

[24] Wiersbe, Warren W. *Be Mature,* 2nd edition. Cook Communications, Ministries, Colorado Springs, CO, 2004, p 29.

[25] Ibid. p. 29.

[26] "Commentary on mask wearing," Fox News. January 2021.

[27] Barclay, William. *The Letters of James and Peter,* revised edition. Philadelphia, The Westminster Press, 1976, p. 45.

[28] Strauss, Lehman. *James Your Brother.* Neptune, New Jersey: Loezeaux Brothers, 1956, p. 18.

[29] A.T. Robertson. *Studies in the Epistle of James.* Nashville, Tennessee: Broadman Press, 1959, p. 41.

[30] "National Debt Clock." www.usdebtclock.org.

[31] Strauss, ibid. p. 19.

[32] Miles, Delos. *Church Growth: A Mighty River.* Nashville, Baptist Sunday Board, 1981.

33 McHenry, R. Comp. *McHenry's Quips, Quotes & Other Notes.* Peabody, Ma. Hendrickson, 1998. Link ac2ldoj.org by Greg Williamson.

34 "Power of An Invite." December 18, 2021. www.churchtrainer.com.

35 Baxter, G. B. *A Leadership Training Manual for the 21st Century Church*, 2011. https://digitalcommons.liberty.edu/cgi/viewcontent.cgi?article=1478&context=doctoral.

36 Harvey, Bonnie C. *D. L. Moody: The American Evangelist.* Uhrichville, Ohio: Barbour, Published 1997.

37 "Paul." *Illustrated Davis Dictionary of the Bible*, p. 612. Nashville, TN: Royal Publishers, Inc., 1973.

38 Goodson, Albert. "We've Come This Far by Faith." Manna Music, Inc., 1965, Renewed 1993.

39 "John Knox is coming! John Knox has come!" www.chosenpeople.com.

40 "Watch: gregorevo." *New Testament Greek Lexicon.* www.biblestudytools.com.

41 "Waiting vs. Watching For Him." Jan. 23, 2011. www.sermoncentral.com. (tag: Second Coming).

42 Stites, Edgar Page, "Trusting Jesus." Public domain.

CPSIA information can be obtained
at www.ICGtesting.com
Printed in the USA
JSHW041405010422
24371JS00002B/7